RECOVER:

"A Woman's Journey from Failure to Restoration"

LaShawanda Moore, MBA, CPC, ELI-MP

RECOVER: "A Woman's Journey from Failure to Restoration"

Contact Information:
www.LaShawandaMoore.com
LaShawanda@LaShawandaMoore.com

ISBN: 978-1-7340082-0-3

Cover Art & Design:
Alfred Lands Creative Design Solutions • alfredlandscds@gmail.com

Interior Art & Layout:
Katie Leary • www.klearydesign.com

Dedication

This book is dedicated to my husband, RodRick Moore, and my four amazing children, RodRick, Jr., Ryan, Randall and London. Thank you for standing by my side, encouraging me, cheering for me, and enduring the test of time throughout my challenges. May God bless you and continue to give you favor wherever you go in life! I love you to the moon and back!

Special Acknowledgments

To my guardian angel, Christina Clark:

Words cannot express the gratitude I have for you. Your mere existence in my life is a God send. Thank you for the vision, belief, encouragement and unconditional love. The execution of this book going out into the world was fueled by your encouragement. May God use it for His glory. Thank you.

To my Uncle, Bishop Alfred T. Lands:

Thank you for the patience, love, belief, encouragement and creativity! I love that my first book has your name on it... Excellence! I love my cover design! I love you.

PART III: Moving On – Turn Your Mess into Your Message

Appendix A:

Appendix B:

Getting the Most from This Book

I wrote this book for women who have endured deep hurt in their work and those who are tired of feeling insignificant, undervalued and excluded. For them, it seems like, no matter how hard they work, they never seem to measure up to the standards and expectations set before them to be successful. They feel stuck where they are, and they know they have so much more to offer; however, they don't know where to begin. Their struggles, pain and hurt have caused them to reach a point of discomfort, where a non-negotiable decision is necessary to move to the next level. Before they can move on, they must recover.

This book is meant to expose the unexposed, bring to light what has been kept in the dark, and to create a space that gives grace to grow from failures and mistakes. This is a daily journey to restoration. At the same time, this book offers an opportunity for intimacy between you and God like never before. The book is divided into three sections:

> **Part I: Feeling the Pain** – In this section, it's okay to sit in your feelings. Don't expect an immediate change in your feelings. Sometimes, the shock of it all takes time for you to process in order to extract value and make sense of it all.

> **Part II: Pruning** – What is God trying to tell you? In this section, consider your situation(s) as lessons to make you better. Even though things may seem unfair, or it may not be your fault, take a moment to step back and look in the mirror to see what you can glean for growth.

Part III: Moving On – Turn your mess into your message. Now that you have learned the lesson, let's learn to think differently. In this section, your test becomes your testimony. This is when implementation of the lesson becomes the reality of your life.

Transformation comes when we read something, meditate, consider ourselves, grab a takeaway or two, then apply what we've learned. Give yourself time to ponder on the content and what God is saying to you before you move on to the next chapter. The greatest impact will come from your own personal application of what is shared. There are five (5) features sprinkled throughout to help you:

- **Lesson** – This will incorporate my story and what I learned from my experience. I will include things that you could consider implementing to help you in your situations.

- **Scripture** – I will incorporate God's Word throughout this book through referencing a Bible story and/or providing applicable Scriptures to meditate on that further enhance the lessons shared.

- **Prayer** – In each chapter, I will pray for you. Prayer changes things, and it is the way we commune with God. As I pray for you, allow the Holy Spirit to ignite prayer within you to deepen your conversation with Him. Only you and the Father truly know your situations, so please add to the prayers as you need to.

- **Meditation** – Here is where I encourage you to take time to sit with the Lord to hear from Him in your spirit.

- **Journaling Exercise** – This will allow you to hear from God and what He is specifically saying to you. Write whatever comes to mind. After you are done with this book, challenge yourself to go back through the book and review what you have written. Email me at LaShawanda@ LaShawandaMoore.com with your testimonies of how

God spoke to you and any subsequent blessings as a result of this book.

One other thing. There is even greater impact if you grab a friend or two, perhaps even a small group, and use this as a guide and conversation starter. You would be surprised at how many other people are going through things that impact them in a deep way, yet they don't have a safe place to share. Let's see if we can create that space and shift the paradigm of one in five adults who experience mental illness. Through my journey, your journey and our conversations with one another, we can do this! Are you ready for the challenge? Let's go!

My Covenant

"Two are better than one, because they have a good return for their labor: If either of them falls down, one can help the other up. But pity anyone who falls and has no one to help them up. Also, if two lie down together, they will keep warm. But how can one keep warm alone? Though one may be overpowered, two can defend themselves. A cord of three strands is not quickly broken."

Ecclesiastes 4:9-12 New International Version (NIV)

With God's help, I commit the next 31 days of my life to deepen my connectivity and intimacy with the Lord such that He speaks to me through my life experiences and uses them for my good.

Your Name: _____

Partner Name(s):

_____

_____

_____

Opening

I started writing this book in April of 2018, during a time in which I was recovering from the deepest hurt in my career. God instructed me to write every day because He was going to use my hurt to help other people. The daily writing helped me process my feelings, and it taught me how to take what was going on and turn it into a great lesson. It also cleansed me from the negative, defeating thoughts from the devil.

It is such a blessing to share this journey from failure to restoration. Yes, you read it right—failure! As I worked on this book, I toiled with the word "failure." There are many perspectives about the word. Whether I failed in some of the situations in my life didn't make me a failure. Did I fail in life? Yes, I have, but the experiences didn't stop me! Did it take me a minute or two to get back up? Yes! It took years sometimes, but I got up!

Understand that failure is not a bad thing. It's not the end all be all. Failure is necessary because it gives us the skills we need to sharpen ourselves. Many people are not transparent enough about their mistakes and failures, and subsequently, how they have managed to overcome. Meanwhile, other people walk around, shattered and broken, thinking they are "failing" alone. They suffer silently. They question themselves and lose who they are because of the situations they've found themselves in.

Additionally, some people are so critical of themselves that they don't give themselves grace and room to make mistakes so they can grow. They stay stagnant and safe, ultimately leaving them complacent and unhappy. Harboring such thoughts and emotions can lead to a feeling of defeat and failure. These thoughts may lead to mental health challenges such as stress, anxiety and depression, which sends people spiraling into a deep pit of darkness. In this darkness, everything and everyone around them is impacted, without their permission.

Studies have shown that one in five adults are experiencing mental health illnesses such as depression, anxiety and stress[1]. In addition, 100 million of the 150 million U.S. workers are doing work that doesn't fulfill them[2]. With these heartbreaking statistics, I believe that intimacy with the Lord and simply having a safe place for conversation can help raise awareness within oneself. Thus, this will motivate them to overcome mental health challenges.

This book was birthed out of my own personal pain, struggle and feelings of shame, false acceptance and false love. I wrote this book as I processed my own mental health challenges of stress and depression. The events over the last five years of my career as a leader were the catalysts that drove me into a deep hurt, which resurrected thoughts of failure, suicide and rejection. Yet, at the same time, it was the catalyst that drove me into self-discovery, reflection and awareness, which now gives me the passion and urgency to share my stories with others, so they realize they are not alone.

This book was first intended for African American women in leadership who have found themselves in extremely hurtful situations in their professional career journey. Yet over time, I realized this is for all women! These are my stories—the struggles of being a brown girl trying to pursue an upward career in corporate America. It was not easy—not so much because of what others were doing to me—but because of what was suppressed within me! The constant awareness of who I am, and why I showed up the way I showed up, became critical to my success.

I am, in no way, bashing corporate America! As I type this, I work in corporate America and I love it! I love the woman I have become as a result of my experiences in corporate. There were several major events,

---

[1] National Alliance on Mental Illness, www.nami.org (2020)
[2] According to Gallup Study, www.gallup.com (2019)

coupled with my buried feelings of my past, that almost took me out of here. But my faith in God, the power of prayer, knowing the Word of God and walking into self-discovery helped me. In addition, I had a circle of influence who was praying and interceding on my behalf during those times.

I will share personal stories, thoughts, prayers, Scriptures, tools and songs I have used to overcome the most difficult events of my life. It is my prayer that you use my life as an example of what God can do for you, as well. I pray that women all over the world will find themselves in this book and take their own personal journey from hurt to restoration. It's time out for us continually feeling like failures. It's time out for being stuck in our wounds and allowing our past to dictate our future. We must utilize all experiences—good and bad—to build the depth and character necessary to go to the next level.

As you read, I want you to read with the following expectations:

1. For God to speak to you

2. To see your own situation differently than you did before reading this book

3. For victory in your life with every page you turn

As you work through this book, you will learn how to spend time at the feet of Jesus as you navigate through your life's trials. Perhaps, you may not be in a hurtful situation right now. You may be reading this out of support of my work, but just hold on to it! Share what you've learned from this book with a friend. Count the people around you. One of them needs it.

Now, don't expect an immediate breakthrough after you read each chapter. Life is a journey! This is a journey! My recovery is still a journey! It takes time to peel back the layers of your life and uncover who you really are and the totality of your purpose.

Let's be clear. Failure is a good thing and it's a necessary thing. It's what catapults us to the next level in life. At every new level, one must endure a valley experience before the mountaintop experience. At each valley experience, you must persevere, endure and maybe even recover as you press on to the next level.

Many times, we pray to God, telling, asking, talking, expressing. However, when do we take time to stop, sit with Him and listen to what He is saying? This was a tough lesson learned for me to add to my "busy" life as a wife, mother of four, leader in corporate America, ministry leader and entrepreneur. Many times, I spent 10-15 minutes of morning "devotion time" and moved on to the next thing to get my day going. Yet, I didn't take the time to absorb what I read. I didn't take time to reflect and allow God to speak to me.

Throughout this book, I will prompt you to sit with God and record what you hear Him say to you. However, feel free to fill each page of this book with the words He is saying to you as you read, with or without my prompting. You may not have more than 15 minutes now, but each incremental minute that you add throughout your entire day will serve you well in your journey with the Lord. The Bible tells us to meditate on His Word day and night; that means to think about His Word all day.

Lastly, it is my prayer that you find peace, hope, encouragement and joy as a result of taking this journey to restoration and recovery with me. My sister, you are a priceless treasure and precious to God. He wants to minister to you through this reading. Sending God's love your way!

A Snippet of My Story

All my life, I never fit in! From being that girl in first grade who wore hunter green pants with a green floral ruffle collared shirt, to my makeshift stacks in my hair, I always stood out. To top it off, my name... La-Sha-wan-da... said it all. Many times, throughout my childhood, I said I was going to change my name as soon as I moved from my mother's house! Oftentimes, I felt rejected and unaccepted by people, teachers and peers, even in my own house. I did not know why I felt this way growing up. My mother loved me with every fiber of her being. So, what more could I want or need?

Because I felt disliked and unaccepted, I competed to be the best in everything. I competed in a pageant and won second runner up, that wasn't good enough for me and so I tried again. Aren't we taught, "if at first you don't succeed, try, try and try again?" My hard work paid off allowing me to be crowned queen. I was also given several opportunities to present my high scoring talent monologue to many different speaking engagements.

In spite of my talent, I continued to "prove" myself to others. I still felt rejection, false love and lack of acceptance throughout high school, into college and well into my engineering career. Issues always arose with people not accepting me for the unique person I was…or did they? Was I making it all up in my mind? Maybe or maybe not.

A portion of my childhood was growing up in a tough environment in Baton Rouge, Louisiana. Drugs, alcohol, sexual promiscuity, and gun shots in the middle of the night were just some of the toxic craziness all around me. Yes, some of it I even participated in. Can you relate to participating in some things you had no business doing? Yet, even though I participated, I knew that wasn't the life I wanted for myself, and definitely not one that my praying mother wanted for me! My mom would always say, "Baby, I want you to go to school, get an education, major in a career that will get you a good paying job, and out of Louisiana." I never forgot those words as I continued on my journey through grade school and into college. In fact, I said yes to a career as a Civil Engineer, surely I would be able to land a good paying job that would get me out of Louisiana. Mind you, while I was in college, I realized that I did not like engineering, but I was convinced that this was the best way to go and get me in the door of a good company with a nice salary. That it did, and with options. I accepted one of my offers working for a major Fortune 500 Company that landed my first job in Victoria, Texas. I made it out!

I had an amazing career traveling the world: Spain, Brazil, France, Taiwan, China, India, Switzerland and many parts of the United States. My diverse jobs included Construction Engineering, Sales, Marketing, Sourcing, Recruiting, Operations, Management, and Six Sigma. I was also featured in a prominent Black engineering magazine. I was receiving many accolades, forming high-level corporate connections, obtaining my MBA and moving up the corporate ladder. But, in 2015, things started to shift. My desire to be an entrepreneur kept tugging at me. My mentors and sponsors started retiring and I found myself in an environment where no one knew my strong positive history. I recognized that my gifts and what I brought to the table were no longer recognized, let alone valued and appreciated. For the first time in my life, the six-figure income, material possessions, spa treatments, nice homes and name brand clothes meant absolutely nothing to me. I found myself in the most depressive state I had ever been. I lost myself in the process of trying to prove myself to others. When I failed to create alliances with the new corporate leaders, I gave in to my inner critic who told me that I wasn't good enough.

There must be a breaking point. I heard someone say, "until the pain of staying the same is greater than the pain of change, you stay the same." Well, when the debacles of life hit me in the last five years of my first career, it was just what the doctor ordered to release me into the next phase of my life.

It was January 2017 when the news hit me like a ton of bricks! I found myself in the center of a debacle that became a major topic of discussion across the entire 3,000-population regional site. I was so embarrassed, weak, hurt, lost, miserable and alone. The hurt was the most excruciating pain that I ever experienced!

For the first time in my career, I was stuck. I could not relocate because I was also opening up a multi-million dollar franchise in the area. This coupled with my strong desire to persevere in the midst of hard times kept me there to change the situation for good. I didn't want to be pushed out.

I wanted to exit with grace. Yet, I was so deeply depressed that there were no words that could describe the inner ache of my heart. I wanted out, in fact, I wanted my life to end. I remember praying to God to just let me die. However, I remembered the call on my life, and that my life was not my own. I remembered my four beautiful children. I had to breakthrough so that I could help others profit from my experience.

God placed on my heart to write through my hurt every day for 30 days. After sharing with my amazing husband, he confirmed and encouraged me to do so. Every morning after my devotion time, I wrote, and Recover was birthed.

In August of 2018, I went away by myself to the mountains of Virginia to be loved on by God…to be restored and to make a humble request. I said, "God, rescue me." I didn't know how I was going to be rescued. Never before in my career was I rated a low performer. I petitioned the Lord and gave Him what I wanted specifically. It was on the day after my birthday, September 7, 2018, I was given the opportunity to exit my first career with grace and step into a new life journey. On October 8, 2018, I started my next career as a full time entrepreneur. Let me tell you, entrepreneurship is not for the faint at heart but, that's a different book!

Today, I am the proud managing owner of a multi-million dollar Franchise. In addition, I am a sought after Transformational Speaker, coach and business consultant as the CEO of Elevate Success. I am now into another career as a senior leader in a Fortune 500 company in the financial sector. My journey has just begun, for I am finally in a place where I can bring my authentic, passionate self to the table each day without judgement. My desire to use my life experiences to help others see what's possible for them has never been more possible than now. I don't regret a single choice made in my life, including becoming an engineer. In fact, my engineering life laid a huge foundation for me and equipped me with tools that serve me well in my current work. My organizational leadership, analytical and problem solving skills play out each day as I take what seems insurmountable and extract value from it. I'm a big fan of engineering and I mentor many others to choose this field of study as a foundation to anything. Has it been easy for a brown girl from the projects of Louisiana? Absolutely not, but it is in the experiences and the journey; the hurt and the pain; and the good and the not so good that builds character and testimonies to serve others along the way. Let me tell you, if I can Recover, so can you. Please know that, recovering isn't a one and done. In fact, you will find that throughout life, you will find yourself repeatedly having to recover from different situations, perspectives and perceptions in order to keep elevating in life.

I am sharing with you what has helped me to continue and recover back to wholeness, so that I own my B.O.L.D. Factor™ daily. No worries, keep going, I'll share with you what that means.

PART I:

Feeling the Pain

Day 1: Oh, But the Shame

I walked into my house after the discussion with Human Resources (HR) and my boss. I was so distraught that I couldn't even look at my children or my husband as I greeted them. I went straight upstairs to the farthest corner in our house, the master bedroom's sitting area, and wept. HR called me in for the first time in my career with accusations that were clearly not my intent. However, the perceptions were the reality to others. Several themes were lodged against me, including making others feel intimidated, religion in the workplace, and not listening to others, to name a few. Clearly these things weren't "bad," but they weren't "good" for someone in leadership, either. This was my first time leading people in corporate America. So, I had much to learn.

I didn't feel like it was a learning opportunity during the time the conversation took place. I felt so hurt because, in my heart, I knew that I only meant well during the six months I had been in the role. I don't intentionally hurt other people. Yet, the people around me were just that—*hurt*. The shame and embarrassment of "messing up" my career overtook me. I just knew I had sabotaged my opportunity to advance and there would be no way to recover. The disgrace and shame consumed my thoughts and peace of mind. I found myself wondering what others thought of me and, most importantly, what my family would think of me for losing my career. The feeling of inadequacy overtook me so much that I felt incapable of recovery.

As I sat there, sobbing profusely, I thought about only one person who could help me in that moment—my spiritual father, Pastor Tony Benson. I took a chance and called him, not thinking he would pick up the phone. But he did! Immediately, he dropped what he was doing. With all the compassion and care he could give, he listened as I shared the embarrassing situation that I found myself. However, I left that conversation feeling loved and empowered to figure out how I could turn this experience into something good. When I left, I believed it was time to get into action. I couldn't stay in my mess or shame.

I needed to realign, engage and organize my thoughts. I had to connect to my purpose and visualize how I wanted the situation to turn out. I needed to equip myself with the Word and release the situation back to God. I was able to take the embarrassment of the situation and turn it into one of the greatest leadership development moments for myself. The first lesson for me was to apologize to my team. I had to ask them to help me turn this thing around because, clearly, I wanted to help our team win. That, my friends, we did. I ended that calendar year in the top performance category and received many accolades for how I handled the situation.

What situation have you experienced in which you felt embarrassment or shame? What if you saw your shame as something that God could use for your *benefit*?

God is a God of grace and mercy.

With time, *He* turns the shame into triumph.

He turns the shame into praise.

He turns the shame into a testimony.

He uses the shame to help others straighten up around you.

He uses the shame to show others His power.

He uses the shame to encourage others that, if you can make it through, so can they.

I know *He* can do it for *you*, just like He did for me!

Take a moment to:

- **R**ealign yourself with who you are and what you know to be true about you.

- **E**ngage your thoughts in a way that controls the toxic beliefs you have formed about the situation.

- **C**onnect to your purpose and to what you are passionate.

- **O**rganize your thoughts to regain control and focus on the mission.

- **V**isualize how you want the situation to turn out and share it.

- **E**quip yourself with the Word to combat the emotions that creep up when you least expect it.

- **R**elease the situation back to God every day and every moment, until you are standing on your story, and not *in* it.

Prayer

God, I thank you for the shame and hurt I feel in this moment; I know that you will use this for my good and your glory. I fear not what others think of me because I know you have redeemed me. Help me to get over myself and to remember that it is not about me, but about what you can do through me. Thank you for forgiving me for the time I fell short. Thank you for helping me see the victory in my situation. Thank you for calling me out by name. Thank you for being with me, even now. I surrender with my hands lifted high and my eyes fixed on you, the author and finisher of my faith. I call it done, in Jesus' name. Amen!

Scriptures for Reflection

Hebrews 12:1-3

Romans 8:31-35

Isaiah 43:1-2

Exercise

Write down your shame right here, because at this moment we're going to leave it on the page. Write your responses underneath each prompt. Take back your power, my friend!

My shame is:

_____

_____

_____

_____

_____

_____

_____

What I know to be true about who I am is:

_____

_____

_____

_____

_____

_____

The toxic beliefs and thoughts that I am getting rid of are:

_____

_____

_____

_____

_____

_____

What I am most passionate about is:

_____

_____

_____

_____

_____

_____

My new thoughts as I reflect on my purpose and passion are:

_____

_____

_____

_____

_____

_____

As a result of my new thoughts, I visualize myself doing:

_____

_____

_____

_____

_____

_____

The Scriptures above spoke the following to me:

_____

_____

_____

_____

_____

_____

_____

I pray that as you responded to each prompt, you experienced a release as if something had been lifted. I also pray that you feel a sense of power as you walk out this day. No worries if you are not totally there yet; this is a journey that we are on together. You may find yourself repeating this process.

Now, let's continue to move forward in your *recovery process*. Take a moment to connect with God.

Meditation

Be still for 5 minutes. Clear your mind. Remember, God speaks in a still, small voice. Listen for Him to speak.

* * *

How did it go? It may feel uncomfortable at first. But as we build this habit, you will crave more special time with your heavenly Father. Take a moment to journal what God said to you.

_____

_____

_____

_____

_____

_____

_____

_____

_____

_____

_____

_____

_____

_____

_____

_____

Day 2: Hold on to Your Confidence

Here we go again, another leadership opportunity! I was so excited to be the new leader of such a huge operation! I looked forward to building upon what the organization had already accomplished, then moving us forward into the company's new strategy. Yet, there was one issue. The organization was upset that I held the leadership position.

I had just finished leading a problem solving meeting with the entire cross functional team. My next meeting was with my peer who was the technical manager at the time. He sat right across from me and I asked: "would you like to meet here in this conference room since we are already in here together?"

Shaking his head side-to-side as in dismay, he responded, "yes, but you need more education." At that moment, I couldn't believe what I heard him say. I could feel the shift in my colleague sitting next to me of discomfort, as I am sure he could not believe what he heard as well.

I asked, "what did you say?" He then began to apologize and state he didn't mean what he said. However, the words were out in the atmosphere, and I heard them. It took everything out of me not to go completely off on him. I began to think about the severity of the situation I was in with this organization just not wanting me there. Not that I was such a bad person, but the entitlement the organization felt for such a position was real.

I remember during a meeting with one of my direct reports, he boldly told me that I was black, didn't know what I was doing, didn't have any experience and it was hard for them to follow my lead. Again, another time of disbelief that a human in the workplace would voice such, although at the same time appreciative of the transparency. I experienced some crushing stuff! Despite the pushback, the rebellion and the lack of acceptance—it was still my responsibility to lead the organization.

How do you gain followership of an organization that doesn't want to follow you? I tried to win them over; but, it wasn't working. The intensity of the situation increased. Things shifted so drastically that I lost myself in the process. Once I realized my loss, I had already failed. When I lost who I was, it became difficult for me to hold on to my confidence to lead. This time, recovery from feeling like a failure was so discouraging that I didn't see a way out. Toxic thoughts crept into my mind, like, *I'm not good enough, smart enough, or polished enough.* Even though I went from feeling excited to be there, to waking up and armoring for battle each day, I learned some things about how to hold on to my confidence and not let go.

When you're battling defeating thoughts, remember that God didn't bring you this far to leave you now. Then understand that we owe no one justification for our existence or our value. Therefore, you want to put into daily practice the following:

1. **Hold your head up toward heaven.** Don't look to your left or to your right. The enemy comes to steal, kill and destroy (John 10:10). As you are looking to the side, he's right there, dangling things in your face to distract you from your mission. When you are in the heat of dodging fiery darts, the position of your head is lowered. Don't give in to the instinct to duck and dodge. Hold your head up high and remember that God is the author and finisher of your faith. He is the beginning and the end. He will have the final say. Therefore, you can walk boldly and confidently in God, knowing He has your back.

2. **Read and meditate on God's promises.** In times of

attack, you need words to speak out loud that will build you from the inside out. Only God's Word can do that for you. Discovering what His Word says about who you are, like being fearfully and wonderfully made (Psalm 139:14), are the very words that will minister to your soul when you need it most. I found myself highlighting a Scripture to use for the day, each day. When I catch myself in the middle of the "stinking thinking" that I'm not good enough, a pattern interrupt is necessary. That interruption is the promises in the Word!

3. **Pray without ceasing.** This is your tool for releasing your pain, hurt and discouragement to the safest place around. God is waiting for you in each moment of the day to love on you, console you and wrap His arms around you. Talk to God and tell Him all about it. Incline your ear to God and let Him assure you that He is there.

4. **Praise God through song.** Nothing is more invigorating than singing your favorite song. This has a way of shifting your energy and thoughts into a place of joy. This just has a way of helping you escape the chaos of life to give our God His due praise. If ever you want to shift your mental state, sing a song of praise.

One of my favorite examples of God using someone who lacked confidence is Gideon. Gideon did not think he was worthy of the task God had for him, but God used him anyway. He even questioned God multiple times to make sure he was the one God wanted to use. Read his story in Judges 6-7.

Exercise

Study Gideon's story to learn the power of God's grace and how He uses the weak to accomplish what seems like the impossible. Gideon gained his strength and confidence from God, and you can, too.

Think of a time you felt prompted by God and you questioned your ability like Gideon did, so much so you needed more confirmation that it was him speaking to you (Judges 6:17). Write it here.

_____

_____

_____

_____

_____

Did you receive confirmation like Gideon, or did you let your faith guide you through?

_____

_____

_____

Take a moment to write down a time when you lacked the confidence to move forward, but you found it within yourself to regain your confidence and press on.

_____

_____

_____

_____

_____

_____

_____

_____

Prayer

God, thank you for giving me gifts and talents that have served me and others well, thus far. When I feel discouraged from comparing myself to others, or because of a mistake, help me to hold on to my confidence in you. You are the one who moves and shapes me. I will not bow to my toxic thoughts, but I will hold on to you. In Jesus' name. Amen.

Scripture for Reflection

Psalm 139:7-17

Meditation

Be still for 5 minutes. Hear God's voice.

* * *

Journal your conversation with God. Let His spirit flow through you as He fills you with the confidence you need to overcome your toxic thoughts.

_____

_____

_____

_____

_____

_____

_____

_____

_____

Day 3: When It Hurts So Bad

Sometimes, my pain was so intense that I went to bed and struggled to stay asleep because of the agony I felt in my chest. I would move and kick my legs, trying to shake it off. I thought that if I kicked or moved hard enough, the thoughts would go away. I thought the pain would subside. When morning came, I didn't want to wake up because I was so tired from the sleepless night. Have you ever felt such severe hurt and pain that you couldn't sleep through the night, and you wake up fatigued?

One morning, I'd had enough of the hurt. I didn't think I had anything left to face the day, let alone face the people at work. As I reflect on this time, I believe I had a lot of these mornings. Yet, on this particular day, I woke up and recalled my restless night. In my mind, I cried out to God, "No! I want it to be over! Just end this, God. Please!" At that moment, I could feel the Holy Spirit trying to comfort me. With this nudging, it helped me lift my head. As I lifted my head, I peeled myself out of bed, part by part. I managed to sit up on the edge of the bed. That was all I had in me. My husband must have noticed my stall. He empathetically told me that it was going to be alright and that I could do it. After all, my husband watched me go through the pain. All he knew to do was to be there for me. Taking in what he said, I realized that if I could just stand, things would feel better; I just needed that initial boost. When I stood up, it was time to armor up and face the giants. I focused on putting one foot in front of the other. With each step of my walk to the bathroom, I called out to God for help.

Each morning, as a part of my devotion, I played worship music to focus more on God, not myself. As a routine, I walked into the bathroom and put the music on to create an atmosphere of praise while I got dressed. This is still my daily routine. Once I made my way to the bathroom, and created my worship atmosphere, I could feel the shifting in my pain. I even felt a release of pressure as I sang. Today, I want to encourage you to find liberty and release in your praise and worship. With the relief is also a feeling of renewal and freshness that can help you press forward.

In the story of Naomi and Ruth, Naomi experienced so much pain and loss in her life that she claimed the name, Mara, which means "bitter" (Ruth 1-2). I can only imagine the hurt she was going through while navigating through life after such loss. I've often wondered how many times Naomi wished she could have blinked and changed things. But she kept it moving anyway.

My friends, when you get to a place where things hurt you so badly, consider lifting your hands and voice in praise. You will be surprised at the level of freedom you immediately feel during that time of praise. It will leave a residual of hope throughout the day that keeps you moving forward.

Exercise

Have you ever experienced so much hurt and pain that you became bitter? How did you move past that pain?

_____

_____

_____

_____

_____

_____

_____

_____

_____

_____

_____

_____

_____

_____

Prayer

When it hurts so bad, bask in the presence of Jesus. Know that the Lord has not forsaken or forgotten you. He will carry you when you can't carry yourself.

Pray with me:

God, thank you for a new day, new mercies and new opportunities to get things right. Comfort me in knowing that you have my back. Help me to let my light shine, even in the midst of my pain. I look forward to the day when it doesn't hurt so badly. In the meantime, I trust you and give you glory. Lord, may my praise be a sweet sound in your ears. In Jesus' name. Amen.

Scriptures for Reflection

2 Corinthians 12:9-10

Isaiah 40:31

Meditation

Quiet your mind for 5 minutes. Set your timer and let the Lord take away your pain.

* * *

Journal your pain. What did God speak to you? Leave it on this page.

_____

_____

_____

_____

_____

_____

_____

_____

_____

_____

_____

_____

_____

_____

_____

_____

_____

_____

_____

_____

_____

_____

_____

_____

_____

_____

_____

_____

_____

_____

_____

_____

_____

_____

_____

_____

_____

_____

_____

_____

_____

Day 4: Be Not Dismayed

When it seems like their plans are succeeding, be not dismayed.

When they think they've got you, be not dismayed.

When it feels like you are all alone and no one is for you, be not dismayed.

When the evil one comes to devour you and eat up your flesh, be not dismayed.

Though it appears an army is against you, be not dismayed.

When your supporters have given up on you, be not dismayed.

When people tell you it's over and you won't recover, be not dismayed.

You see, my sisters, I have experienced this level of darkness on more than one occasion. It was September 2017 when I had enough. I had attended the Authentic Ladies International Prayer Breakfast. During the session, the leader stated, "There are no unspoken requests." I heard her say it the first time; she repeated it again. I didn't really know the women in the room, but I felt this amazing safety come over me. I raised my hand and said, "I have an unspoken request." The leader then created the space for me to pour out my heart and my desire to be rescued from my current job. I was in such deep anguish and depression that I could no longer stay there. I was sick and tired of being treated like I was dumb and worthless by the people around me. I was fed up with being talked about and lied on. I was done with people not respecting me for what I brought to the table.

I cried out so loudly and boldly to the Lord, and those women gathered around me in the most heartfelt prayer they could pull from their bellies. They laid hands on me, ministered to me, and assured me that God heard my prayer. That's when I got up off the floor. Yes, I was face down on the floor. I dried my face, got myself together and walked away, believing my help was on the way. I got such peace from that day that I was able to focus on being who God wanted me to be right where I was, without question. It was exactly one year later that the Lord answered my prayer and rescued me from the chains that kept me shackled from flourishing the way He ordained me.

Psalm 37:1 says, *Do not be concerned about the evildoers around you and the schemes that appear to succeed on their behalf.* Instead, I want you to cry out to the Lord the ugliest cry you could ever muster. Walk away, believing that God has you! In every dark place I have been in, each time, the Father showed up and rescued me from my enemies. God enabled me to hold my head up high with a smile on my face. He comforted me and reminded me to whom I belonged. When you are the King's kid, no worries; fret not yourself of evildoers. You, too, can be rescued from the battle with your enemies! God's got the last word!

Whenever you are working in God's will to accomplish your purpose, there will be skeptics. Jesus had them with the Pharisees. Daniel had them with the royal administrators who envied his favor with King Darius. They preyed on the only thing Daniel would never waver in—his faith in God. By issuing a decree outlawing prayer for 30 days, they knew they had Daniel exactly where they wanted him (Daniel 6:1-12).

Daniel's faith in God was greater than the fear of his enemies. He did not let a royal decree prevent him from praising and communicating with his heavenly Father. And, what was his punishment? He was thrown into the lion's den. His enemies plotted his demise, but God protects His children. God shut the mouths of the lions. (Daniel 6:16-24) What lion's mouth do you think He can shut for you?

Exercise

Can you recall a time when you were being attacked by your enemies, like Daniel? How did your faith in God restore you?

_____

_____

_____

_____

_____

_____

_____

Daniel's faith was tested by his enemies, and yours will be tested, as well. Use Daniel's example to stay strong and committed to God amidst the battle. Your Father will protect you, as He protected Daniel.

Prayer

Father, I thank you for having my back. Thank you for fighting my battles and taking care of vengeance. Help me to remember that, no matter what it looks like, you have the final say. I am not dismayed. In Jesus' name. Amen.

Scriptures for Reflection

Psalm 37

Psalm 23

Meditation

Listen for God's still, small voice. Set a timer for 5 minutes and meditate.

* * *

Journal God's words to you. He will deliver you from the hands of your enemies. Cling to His light.

_____

_____

_____

_____

_____

_____

_____

_____

_____

_____

_____

_____

_____

_____

_____

_____

_____

Day 5: Let My Light Shine

"Let my light shine so that others may see you" is a prayer I pray quite often. No matter how bad I feel about myself, or what is happening in my life, I want God to conceal those things from an external view and allow the God in me to shine through. At work, the one thing people say about me is that I'm always smiling. I get it from my mama. No matter what was going on in her life, she always kept a smile on her face.

When someone asked her how she was doing, her response was always, "Wonderful!" I couldn't understand how she could say that all the time because I knew what was happening in her life. The older I got, the more I realized that she'd taught me a valuable lesson. She said, "When you say you feel wonderful, you can't help but feel differently and smile as you put it out into the atmosphere. When you put it out there, it lifts your spirit and gives you hope." Well, guess who started answering, "Wonderful!" whenever someone asked, "How are you doing?" Just that one word made a difference in my thoughts and uplifted the other person who asked me how I was doing. Somehow, they were encouraged; I could tell by their response.

However, there was a season when I lost that response. Oddly enough, it was after I was liberated from working a corporate job to becoming a full-time entrepreneur. The stress of trying to figure out my new life, and how I could consistently bring in income, suppressed my consciousness of being wonderful. There is a lesson here. Letting your light shine has nothing to do with an external response. It's about an internal connection with the author of our joy. The joy of the Lord is our strength. When you have joy, there is nothing no one, or no situation, can do to steal it from you. Therefore, rather than forcing an external way of being, spend time being filled with the joy of the Lord. Then, and only then, will the light of the Lord shine through you.

Once you are filled daily from the inside, the smile and your response of, "Wonderful!" will come across much more authentically. After all, you never know what others are going through in their lives. As Christians, we may be the only light others see. No matter what or how bad you feel, don't miss the opportunity to lift someone else up with the presence of the Lord. It just might make you feel better in the process.

Ruth was a woman who exuded love in the Bible. After losing her husband at a young age, she decided to cleave to her mother-in-law, despite her mother-in-law's plea to move on and restart her life (Ruth 1:17). Ruth was the "wonderful" in Naomi's life. Despite the bitterness that Naomi adopted, Ruth chose to love her and joyfully bind herself to her.

Have you ever found yourself in a bitter situation, yet, you chose to feel joy and encourage those around you despite your challenges? That's what Ruth did! Share your story.

Exercise

Smile.

How did it feel? Speak the words: *I feel wonderful.*

Listen to the song, "I Smile" by Kirk Franklin. This song ministers to me every time I listen. It reminds me that we don't have to look like what we are going through. Put a smile on your face and ignite that spark from within. God gave it to you so you can shine it on others. Jesus is the best example of light on earth. Follow His example (Matthew 5:16).

How are you feeling? Write it here.

_____

_____

_____

_____

_____

_____

_____

_____

_____

Prayer

Lord, thank you for your Son who suffered, bled and died for me. There is no greater hurt than what Jesus experienced. Help me to be reminded that even in His hurt, Jesus thought about others. May my light shine so that others are lifted. In Jesus' name. Amen.

Scriptures for Reflection

Proverbs 23:7

James 1:2

Galatians 5:22

Proverbs 18:21

Isaiah 60:1

Meditation

Quiet your mind. Meditate with the Lord for 5 minutes. Let His light shine through you.

* * *

Journal your time with the Lord. He will give you the strength to shine and reflect His glory.

_____

_____

_____

_____

_____

_____

_____

_____

_____

_____

_____

_____

_____

_____

_____

_____

_____

Day 6: Show Me a Sign

Have you ever felt like God wasn't there? Have you ever felt like He doesn't hear your prayers? Or maybe you just couldn't feel His presence in your life? This feeling often leads to feeling alone. It is painful when you are amid a storm or trying to be restored. I have a vivid memory of a point in my career where I felt this way. It was after a major fall. Typically, when you go through a difficulty in your career, your mentors are there to help guide you through. However, at this time in my career, most of my mentors and people who would vouch for me had left the company.

It became increasingly important to build new relationships with people of influence. This task was extremely difficult, especially when I allowed my toxic thoughts to control my decisions. I assumed everyone knew about my failure and had formed an opinion about my lack of capability. Most of the leaders I was working to connect with were either new to the business or new to the company. They came in during my 19th year with the company—the worst year of my career!

They knew nothing of my past and how strong of a performer I was. No matter what, they had no past basis. No matter how hard I tried to connect, I felt stuck. It felt like a dead end for me. I felt alone. I couldn't feel the hand of God upon me. One day, I asked God to please show me a sign that He hears me and that I'm not in the storm alone. I kid you not, that day one of the leaders I was trying to connect with reached out to me with an opportunity to help another site. This was a perfect opportunity to do what I enjoyed the most while demonstrating my capability to someone who was not familiar with my performance. But God!

I knew that this was an answer to my prayer. The favor of the Lord was upon me. I immediately thanked Him because He hastened unto me just when I needed to see some sign that He was near. Amid my trial, He was with me.

Imagine the trial that Hannah experienced as she longed for a child. The Bible said that she was subjected to taunting to the point that she refused to eat (1 Samuel 1:7). Yet, God had a plan for her life. After a desperate prayer to God, she put her hurt aside and leaned on the favor of the Lord. Sounds familiar? The Bible doesn't reveal how long after her prayer she conceived, but she knew God was faithful. Sometimes, we must press through the pain and realize that God is in control and will remain faithful.

Have you ever prayed fervently to God and expected a change? The Bible doesn't reveal how long Hannah remained bitter about her childless situation, or how long she prayed. But something happened on her trip to Shiloh. Hannah decided to lay her burdens on the Lord and trust Him to see it through (1 Samuel 1:9-19).

Do you see what happened when Hannah put her full trust in the Lord and released her anxieties? The Scripture says, "The Lord remembered her." Don't take your prayers for granted. *He* hears everything you tell him. *He* is always connected, and *He* is always listening. Be patient and wait on Him to deliver. Hannah's patience yielded a very special son—Samuel! Read her full story in 1 Samuel 1.

As a child of God, He promised victory in all situations. No matter what the situation looks like, or how dim the future looks, this is the time that we lean into the only source. Hold on to God's unchanging hand. Know that we can always trust God. He will always have our best interest in mind. Just ask Him to show you a sign that He is there, and He will. Be sure to pay close attention because, if you are not careful, you can miss Him!

Exercise

Can you think of a time in your life when you felt like God showed you a sign? Do you recall a time when you decided to rest and place your trust in the Lord to see you through a difficult situation like Hannah? What was the result?

_____

_____

_____

_____

_____

_____

_____

_____

_____

Prayer

God, I need to hear from you. I need to feel you. I need to see your hand in this situation. Please show me a sign that you got me and are working things out for me. In Jesus' name. Amen.

Scriptures for Reflection:

Exodus 33:14

Jeremiah 29:13

John 14:16

Meditation

Be still. Set your timer for 5 minutes. Feel God's presence. He has not left you.

* * *

Journal your time with the Lord. What signs has He shown you?

_____

_____

_____

_____

_____

_____

_____

_____

_____

_____

_____

_____

_____

_____

_____

_____

_____

_____

Day 7: Basking in Your Presence

During one of the most difficult times in my life, the pain of my failure lingered each day. It took much effort and initiative to hold my head up high. The ease of simply succumbing to my ill feelings, and wanting to escape from the chaos of life, was real. It felt as though no one or nothing could relieve me of the agony I was experiencing. In fact, I vividly remember trying to figure out how I could take my life and be excused from the pain.

One Thursday evening, I was trying to prepare mentally, spiritually and emotionally for my Bible study group that met in my home weekly. Frankly, I just couldn't do it that night. I called one of our sisters in Christ and asked if she could teach. Of course, she agreed. That night during study, I sat there as a zombie, but as one with tears. As I looked at each of them, all I could think was that surely none of them would ever get themselves into something so deep and impactful to their careers, lives and families as I had. I wept bitterly that evening during Bible study. I hated to put that on the ladies, but they simply prayed and rubbed my back. One even said how much she hated to see me like that. In the moment, I knew that, as the leader of the study, I had to get it together. When I decided to put my burdens down and bask in His presence, it made things easier to bear.

I say to you, "Lift your head up, my sister!" Turn on your worship music. Start your morning with prayer and Scripture, then watch God move you from, "Woe is me" to "Woe, why not me?" He will turn your sorrow into joy, your pain into triumph, and your tears into laughter. Take this day to bask in the presence of God. Know that He is your Father and you are His daughter. Imagine Him lifting you up in the air, looking into your eyes, smiling and spinning you around, just like a small child. I never experienced this on earth, but I have placed myself in the arms of my heavenly Father and felt this wonderful feeling of love, safety and comfort.

Exercise

Paul and Silas basked in the presence of the Lord while imprisoned in chains. And, do you know what happened? A miracle—God opened the prison doors! (Acts 16:24-36) We are not beyond miracles today.

Describe a time when you chose to bask in the presence of the Lord like Paul and Silas. How did it feel?

_____

_____

_____

_____

_____

_____

_____

_____

_____

_____

_____

_____

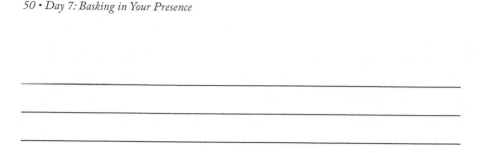

Prayer

Heavenly Father, I'm so glad to be your daughter. In times when my heart is so heavy, I know I can come to you and lay in your lap. Help me to place myself in this moment all day and bask in your presence. In Jesus' name. Amen.

Scriptures for Reflection

Psalm 98:4-6

Psalm 47:1-2

2 Samuel 12:20

Songs for Reflection

Here is a list of some of my favorite worship songs I turn to when I just need to bask in His glory. Take some time to listen.

"Before the Throne" by Shekinah Glory Ministries

"Your Presence is Heaven" by Israel Houghton & New Breed

"All I Want is You" by William McDowell

"Lord I Need You" by Matt Maher

Meditation

After you've listened to some praise music, silence the room for 5 minutes. Be still. Listen for God's voice. Connect.

* * *

Document your time with God. What is He communicating to you? Empty your words on the page.

_____

_____

_____

_____

_____

_____

_____

_____

_____

_____

_____

_____

_____

_____

_____

_____

_____

Day 8: Peace Be Still

In Matthew 8, after a long day of performing miracles, Jesus got into a boat and His disciples followed Him. Not too long after, the sea became so rough that the ship was covered with waves amid a windy storm (Matthew 8:24). All the while, Jesus was still asleep. However, the disciples were scared nearly to death. They just knew they would die in the storm. They cried out, "Lord, save us! We are perishing!" Then Jesus asked them, "Why are you fearful, O you of little faith?" Then He stood up and calmed the sea (Matthew 8:25-26).

How many times have you felt like you were perishing during the storms of life? In those moments, you looked for help because it seemed like the experience was more than you could handle. Yet, in the right time—God's time, which happens to be on time—He reached out His hand and calmed things around you. As you reflect, I encourage you to ask God for another time like that. In fact, right now, ask Him to give you a peace that only He can give. The peace that quiets the windy storms of life around you. The kind where human beings can't fathom why you would be at such peace when they see the chaos going on around you. The Word says, *"If you abide in me, and my words abide in you, you will ask what you desire, and it shall be done for you"* (John 15:7). How often do you remember to ask for peace?

Sometimes, we get so caught up in what is physically around us that we forget to call on the One who is divinely over us all. All we must do is cry out for help, and He will come through, declaring, "Peace, be still!" (Mark 4:39). And that it will be. Once you pray this prayer, believe and walk into peace.

Prayer

God, please save me from this suffering and chaos around me. I don't know if I'm coming or going because the enemy is taking over. Save me, God! Restore me so that I may serve more. Give me peace that only you can give—the peace that surpasses all understanding. Amen.

Exercise

How are you tapping into the peace that God provides?

_____

_____

_____

_____

_____

_____

_____

Scriptures for Reflection

Philippians 4:6-7

1 Peter 5:6-7

Songs for Reflection:

"It is Well with My Soul" by any artist

"Great is Thy Faithfulness" by any artist

Meditation

Set your timer for 5 minutes. Quiet your mind.

* * *

Take a moment to think about what you read today and write down what is coming up for you. How can you use this day's reading for your own situation?

_____

_____

_____

_____

_____

_____

_____

_____

_____

_____

_____

_____

_____

_____

_____

_____

_____

PART II:

Pruning – What is God Trying to Tell You?

Day 9: Encourage Yourself

Looking back on the hard times in my career, it felt like I failed. I was done! Stick a fork in me! Never in my life had I felt like such a failure. I felt like I'd let down my mentors, my family, my husband, my children—all those who believed in me. It was truly embarrassing. In fact, all I had put into my career—hard work, sweat and tears—seemed to have vanished before my very eyes.

During this time, some days I woke up, refreshed and ready to conquer the day. Other days, not so much. I can vividly remember the time when I just couldn't get up! There was nothing inside me to pull myself out of the bed. I cried out to my husband to help me! He came around to my side of the bed and pulled me up to my feet. It was not easy getting me up because my body and mind held me down. Yet, he kept at it until I stood up. And when I stood up, I wiped away the tears and put one foot in front of the other. I realized I could make it if I kept stepping. My husband went on to work as I continued to get dressed.

Sister, I want you to know that you can make it. It just takes a press after a little pull. The pull, in this case, was my husband. The press was my forward motion. Once I got going and turned on my praise music, I encouraged myself. You see, sometimes you must encourage yourself, especially in those times of deep hurt and pain. Whatever it takes, hold your head up high and remember that God has the final say. No one has the authority over you, but God. Lift your head and press today.

As you move today, remember we are in a pruning process consistently. Everything happens for a reason. He's only deepening your character and developing the woman He needs you to be in the next season. Sometimes, you must speak life into your situation and into *yourself*. You can't rely on someone else to do all the work. Once my husband left for work, I was left to reach inside myself to continue stepping. As I stepped, I praised; as I praised, I believed. As I believed, I took another step. Believe in God and yourself. Together, there is nothing that can stop you or keep you down! Try it today. I love you, my sister. You can do it!

Prayer

Lord, I am your child. You know all about me. You know how much my heart aches. Lord, I'm looking to you in this moment to help me to keep putting one foot in front of the other. As I step, help me to hold my head up in confidence that I can make it. Help me to learn the lessons and to build from the inside so that you always get the glory out of my life. Amen.

Let's step back into the story of Esther for a moment. Do you think she had to encourage herself? Mordecai placed the burden and responsibility on her shoulders of saving her entire race! That's a heavy weight to carry. Going before the king without being summoned could have cost Esther her life. Don't you think she needed to encourage herself before undertaking this enormous task? (Esther 4:15-16)

Exercise

Have you had to encourage yourself before undertaking something big? What things do you like to do to encourage yourself?

_____

_____

_____

_____

_____

_____

_____

_____

_____

_____

_____

_____

Scriptures for Reflection

Philippians 4:13

2 Corinthians 12:7-10

Song for Reflection

"Encourage Yourself" by Donald Lawrence & The Tri-City Singers.

Meditation

Set your timer for 10 minutes. Quiet your mind.

* * *

Take a moment to think about what you read today and write down what is coming up for you. How can you use this day's reading for your own situation?

_____

_____

_____

_____

_____

_____

_____

_____

_____

_____

_____

_____

_____

_____

_____

_____

_____

_____

_____

Day 10: Looking for Growth Opportunity

Have you ever felt like the circumstances you were put in caused you to fail? Have you ever felt that if X had not happened, you would not have Z? In those situations, do you feel people deceived others about you, and that your reactions were not intended the way they were perceived? To top it off, your heart was pure the entire time! There was a time when it seemed like people perceived everything about me negatively. It felt like others totally misread me, and it was being held against me. I knew in my heart that my intentions were good, but the department already had a negative perception of me.

One of the things lodged against me was "I micromanaged and did not listen to others." One thing my experience has taught me is that, in every situation, there is a lesson to learn and an opportunity to grow. Rather than getting caught up in questioning, "Why me?" or proving myself, I looked at what I had done to cause the perception. I also looked at what I should do differently in the future. We all make mistakes; yet, the hope is that we don't make the same mistakes again. The Bible says, *And not only that, but we also glory in tribulations, knowing that tribulation produces perseverance; and perseverance, character; and character, hope. Now hope does not disappoint, because the love of God has been poured out in our hearts by the Holy Spirit who was given to us* (Romans 5:3-5, NKJV).

What if we looked at every situation as an opportunity to build character that is necessary to take us to the next level? What if we looked at situations in a different light? I want to offer you this perspective. During times like these, look in the mirror and ask yourself these questions:

1. Why do others view me this way?

2. What is the common theme?

3. What can I do to change things?

Take personal ownership without being defensive. Ask God to show you what He is developing in you as a result of this situation. This introspective process will allow you to focus on your growth and build depth of character.

What do you think God was trying to teach David when he was fleeing for his life from King Saul? Here was David, the anointed future king of Israel, running for his life. I'm sure he didn't think he deserved this fate, but he remained humble. David stayed faithful and waited on God (1 Samuel 23-24).

Exercise

Growth is often painful, but a necessary process. In the midst of our storm, it's hard to see the lesson God is trying to teach us.

Think of a particularly difficult season that helped you grow into who you are. How did you learn and grow from it?

Prayer

God, amid this trial, help me to see clearly what you are cultivating and changing to build fortitude for my future. As you open my eyes, give me clear direction so that each word I say, and each thing I do, demonstrates growth. In Jesus' name. Amen.

Scripture for Reflection

Romans 5:3-5

Meditation

We are positioning ourselves for growth, which means we are now ready to spend more intimate time with the Lord. Set your timer for 10 minutes. Quiet your mind and listen for what He has to say.

* * *

God wants to use your challenges and obstacles to promote growth. What is He pruning you for? What did God tell you today?

_____

_____

_____

_____

_____

_____

_____

_____

_____

_____

_____

_____

_____

_____

_____

_____

_____

Day 11: Work as Unto the Lord

There was a time when I was so busy trying to meet the expectations of others and prove myself, that I lost my focus on who I was and who I was really working for. I lost myself completely. Soon after transitioning to a new job, and transitioning into a new function in the company, that's when I took a second look in the mirror. Since this was my first time working in operations, I felt like the people took a chance on me. As you can imagine, this created a lot of stress and pressure to perform. The difficult part was that many people around me were not open to me coming from corporate headquarters and becoming their leader. They knew I had no experience in the job function.

It was a tough environment and culture to break through. When I stepped back to look at what I could learn from the situation, I realized I needed to remember who I was and who I belonged to. I needed to recalibrate and remember that I wasn't there working for man. I was working as unto the Lord. I took inventory of my strengths and used that to help me dissect the needs of the organization.

My situation was complicated and too long of a story for this short segment. So, my message is to remember that, no matter what happens, as a child of God, you are victorious. You have everything within you to succeed. Keep your eyes fixed on the source of your help and pray consistently for guidance. Work as unto the Lord, giving Him your best. It is my plea and prayer that you do not lose yourself in your situation. Be clear on the vision and expectations of your leader. Build relationships all around you, and work with them to gain wins that get results for the business.

This reminds me of the story of Esther. She did not grow up expecting to be queen. She embraced a new role of royalty that positioned her to save her people. Mordecai reminded her of her duty when he told her, *"And who knows but that you have come into your royal position for such a time as this?"* (Esther 2-10).

Exercise

What is God preparing you for? Esther was placed into the role of queen to save her people. What do you feel God is calling you to do?

_____

_____

_____

_____

_____

_____

_____

Prayer

God, thank you for every opportunity to use my gifts for your glory. Help me to not work as unto men, but to work as unto you. May I meet your standards and expectations as I'm reminded of your grace. For I know your grace is sufficient. In Jesus' name. Amen.

Scripture for Reflection

Colossians 3:23-24

Meditation

Quiet your mind. Be quiet for 10 minutes and listen to God's voice. What does He want to tell you?

* * *

Journal your prayer time. What did the Lord share with you today?

_____

_____

_____

_____

_____

_____

_____

_____

_____

_____

_____

_____

_____

_____

_____

_____

_____

_____

_____

Day 12: Attitude of Gratitude

Are you tired of feeling defeated, sad and hurt? When you've been through so much, it takes all your energy to keep going. But, you must. As a Christian, Satan wants us to be discouraged and overtaken by grief. Yet, we can't give him an inch of glory! The mind is powerful, and we can ignite our power at any moment by choosing our frame of reference. You can turn things around in your head by waking up each morning with an attitude of gratitude. You set the tone for your day. Spending the quiet time with God, then taking some time to think about the great things in your life, can transform your stinking thinking to gratefulness.

I challenged my Connected Women in Christ Bible study group to go 21 days writing down ten things they love about themselves and to post in the group. This process was therapeutic. I was experiencing a trial where I felt undervalued, disrespected and not good enough. That writing assignment helped me reflect on the good versus the trials. I was able to operate from a deeper place and connectivity with myself, and who God created me to be.

Once we completed the 21 days, this writing assignment became a fulfilling habit. I transitioned to writing ten things I was grateful for each morning. Friends, this set my mind in a positive, victorious space each day. Now, I hold my head up and walk into my victory each day. God wants us to give thanks unto Him and show Him how much we appreciate Him. He wants us to acknowledge Him and to adore Him. Practicing daily gratitude journal writing made it easier to bless Him, while at the same time, restoring my joy.

This reminds me of the story of the ten lepers in the book of Luke. Ten lepers asked Jesus to have mercy on them and heal them, and He did. After receiving their healing, nine of them went their separate ways. But one returned to Jesus to praise Him and show gratitude. His thankfulness moved Jesus (Luke 17:11-19). Imagine what yours can do.

Exercise

Being thankful has power in your life. Can you remember a time when you felt defeated, yet chose to reflect on gratitude to shift your thinking? How did this change your perspective?

_____

_____

_____

_____

_____

_____

_____

_____

_____

_____

_____

List 10 things you are grateful for:

1. _____

2. _____

3. _____

4. _____

5. _____

6. _____

7. _____

8. _____

9. _____

10. _____

That wasn't so hard, was it? Do you think you can do this for 30 days? Wake up and appreciate what you are grateful for. It will change your perspective, especially when you're going through a storm. Will you commit to an attitude of gratitude?

Prayer

Lord, help me to be reminded of how blessed I am, even in times of deep struggle. Help me to get out of "woe is me" mode to an attitude of gratitude mode. Let the joy of the Lord beam from me. In Jesus' name. Amen.

Scripture for Reflection

Psalm 107:1

Meditation

Give the Lord 10 minutes of silence. Listen for Him.

* * *

Journal your time with the Lord. Continue to express your gratitude and how you can bring Him glory through your joy.

_____

_____

_____

_____

_____

_____

_____

_____

_____

_____

_____

_____

_____

_____

_____

_____

_____

_____

_____

Day 13: Show Me Myself

On April 14, 2018, I ran a 10K. I began training for the race well in advance; however, five weeks prior to race day, I hurt my Achilles tendon. I had to stop running for a while. Race day came, and I wanted to run all 6.2 miles. My strategy was to pace myself and keep moving. The first half was great, even up to the mile-four marker. But getting to the mile-five marker took forever! Once I hit mile five, I thought, *Only one left to go and I'll speed up closer to the finish line.* I noticed a white banner across the race area above and I assumed it was the finish line. I sped up. I looked around and noticed people passing me who appeared to be in less shape than I was. I kicked myself into another gear and sped up.

Two things happened at this point:

1. I noticed the banner wasn't the finish line.

2. I got tired and I wanted to stop.

Those people kept running ahead of me. I couldn't understand how they were able to keep going so strong. Then, a portion of Ecclesiastes 9:11 came to my mind: *The race is not given to the swift or the battle to the strong...* I just needed to endure until the end.

It occurred to me that, just like in life, I can't look to my left or right and compare my life's journey to others. I don't know their situation. Each time I compare, I get distracted and it takes me off course. Instead, I need to keep my eyes fixed on Jesus. I must stay focused on the true finish line and run my own race.

Choose to stop comparing yourself to others' perceived success. Focus on what God wants to show you during your journey. I would always ask God, "Show me *me*" during my trials, struggles and pain. I always wanted to come out better. Better is always a winner.

Recall the story of Rachel and Leah. Can you imagine having to share your husband with your sister? That's what these two had to endure. To make matters worse, Jacob loved Rachel more than Leah, which weighed heavy on her self-worth. They had to constantly fight comparison to gain the attention and love of Jacob in their household. Their great reward in the end was that they both become the mothers of the twelve tribes of Israel. Read their story in Genesis 29-30.

Exercise

You must run your own race, not someone else's. Describe a time in your life when you allowed comparison to weigh you down. How did God show you yourself so that you could emerge from the situation and know your worth?

_____

_____

_____

_____

_____

_____

_____

_____

_____

_____

_____

_____

_____

_____

_____

_____

_____

_____

_____

Prayer

Lord, thank you for helping me to refocus on you as I navigate through life's journey. Help me to see myself and improve my life technique along the way. In Jesus' name. Amen.

Scriptures for Reflection

2 Timothy 4:7

Galatians 5:7

Hebrews 12:1

Meditation:

Quiet your mind. Set your timer for 10 minutes. Ask God what race you need to focus on in your life. Let Him help you stay focused. Now, listen.

* * *

Journal your conversation with God. What did you learn today?

_____

_____

_____

_____

_____

_____

_____

_____

_____

_____

_____

_____

_____

_____

_____

_____

_____

_____

Day 14: Help Me Focus on Serving

Thank God for the people He has placed in my life. Remember I told you I started and led a women's ministry, Connected Women in Christ, in which we held a weekly Bible study in my home. At the onset of my huge career trial in January 2017, I was in such a horrible place. I felt like a victim and my energy level declined. I knew I couldn't stay in a defeated state and serve them the way in which they needed to be served. After all, they were counting on me to show them how to get through hardships with faith. I must admit, in the beginning, there were times when I could not facilitate the sessions. Instead, I just wanted to sit, cry and listen. I wanted others to feel sorry for me.

Yes, my sister, I wanted pity. Most importantly, I wanted to be prayed for and loved on. I wanted to hear that it would be okay. Believe me, they loved on me when I needed it most. In fact, some Thursdays, I was so broken that I could not facilitate the study. I immediately called on a sister to facilitate. She accepted, without hesitation. Then, there were other days that I just couldn't do it. Once again, I called on another sister to facilitate. She too, without hesitation, stepped in.

I share this with you because, during this time, I learned a valuable leadership lesson in ministry. It became apparent that, as a leader, my calling is to develop others and to give them an opportunity to use their gifts. My storm created an opportunity for others to prepare, speak, lead and facilitate the Bible study. There are so many gifted women in my group. This was the perfect time to let them share. At the same time, I received ministry. They loved on me and prayed for me.

During times of pain and suffering, we still must lead. We still must put the organization and team before ourselves. We cannot forsake our role because we are hurt. As we get caught up in focusing on others, guess what? It takes your mind off of self.

Deborah was a great example of leadership and servitude in the Bible. For sure, she endured challenges of her own as the first female judge noted in the Bible (Judges 4).

Exercise

Describe a leadership position where you were called to serve. How did it feel? Did you ever have a time in which you had to shift your focus back to developing others? How did you do it?

_____

_____

_____

_____

_____

_____

_____

_____

_____

_____

_____

Our call is to serve the Lord. This includes serving His people. Today, I challenge you to take your mind off yourself and focus on serving. Who can you serve today?

_____

_____

_____

_____

_____

_____

_____

_____

_____

_____

Prayer

Lord, in my hurt, help me to honor my call as a leader to serve and develop others. Don't let me stay stuck in my feelings. Help me to remember those who are counting on me to lead the way. Continue to heal my heart in the background. At the end of the day, may you get the glory out of this experience. In Jesus' name. Amen.

Scriptures for Reflection

Ephesians 6:7

Meditation

Listen for Him. Silence your mind for 10 minutes as He tells you where you need to serve.

* * *

Journal your prayer. Where can you serve and heal in the process?

_____

_____

_____

_____

_____

_____

_____

_____

_____

_____

_____

_____

_____

_____

_____

_____

_____

_____

_____

_____

Day 15: Guard My Thoughts

Each day that I wake up with breath in my body, I'm grateful. I'm ready to have a great day. No matter what, I try to welcome a fresh perspective on my day. *However*, there were a few trials I faced in my life that caused me to want to take my life! In fact, it was one Sunday morning when my stepfather and I fell out. Whether it was true or not, it felt like no one heard me in my home and no one favored me.

In my junior year of high school, I had enough! I went into the bathroom, opened the medicine cabinet, and emptied every bottle of prescribed medicine I could find into my body. My stepfather had back issues, so there was plenty of prescription medicine available. We went to church and I must have stumbled out of the sanctuary during the service. The last thing I remembered that day was sitting at the table with my mom and sister, trying to eat a Whopper from Burger King. The next morning, I woke up in the hospital with black chalk all over me. My pastor was sitting by my bedside.

Fast forward many years later, even after having children, thoughts of suicide crept into my mind. It always seemed like an option when the going got tough. During the last five years of my first career in corporate America, I wanted to leave this earth! Given my circumstances, it wasn't easy standing strong and keeping a smile on my face, but I did in public. Although I wore a smile on the outside, on the inside, I was slowly dying. I allowed toxic thoughts to take over my mind, reading into situations based upon assumptions, which ultimately made things worse. The mind is powerful! We can make or break ourselves simply by our thoughts. When we are hurting, negative thinking easily creeps into our minds.

We look for signs to validate our thinking. If you look for the negative, you will find the negative. If you look for the positive, you will find the positive. Whatever we believe in our heart about ourselves, it will show up outwardly in our actions and beliefs. In one season of my life, I had to develop daily "I am" affirmations to set the tone for my thoughts. This exercise, along with positive self-talk, helped me make it through each day. When a negative thought came, I replaced it with a positive thought.

Are your thoughts eating you alive? Are your thoughts causing you to draw conclusions or make up stories that aren't facts? Jot some of those thoughts down here.

_____

_____

_____

_____

_____

When Jesus was in the wilderness and taken up to a mountain, Satan tried to tempt Him. He was trying to penetrate His thoughts. But Jesus fought the enemy with Scripture, which is the most powerful weapon we have (Matthew 4:1-11).

Exercise

The Book of Proverbs is packed with positive affirmations to grow your self-image; yet, one of my favorites is Proverbs 31: 10-31. Read this passage of Scripture and imagine yourself as a "Proverbs 31 Woman." What kind of thoughts do you believe she had about herself?

_____

_____

_____

_____

_____

_____

Pause right now and think of the good things about yourself and others around you. Here are some of the positive affirmations that I say to myself. You will want to develop your own. But for now, say these:

> I am love.
>
> I am peace.
>
> I am patience.
>
> I am fearfully and wonderfully made.
>
> I am a great leader.
>
> I am kindness.
>
> I am confidence.
>
> I am hope.
>
> I am healed.
>
> I am power.

After all, if you don't believe these things for you, who else will?

Prayer

Lord, help me to guard my thoughts today and get rid of the negative thinking that corrupts my actions, behaviors and responses to my surroundings. Help me to think on good, positive and true things all day. Heighten my awareness when my thoughts go astray so that I make quick changes. In Jesus' name. Amen.

Scripture for Reflection

Philippians 4:8

Meditation

Clear your mind of the clutter. Talk to God for a few minutes. Set your timer to 10 minutes.

* * *

Journal your time with God. Release those toxic thoughts right here on this page, if you need to. Get them out of your head to make room for good thoughts.

_____

_____

_____

_____

_____

_____

_____

_____

_____

_____

_____

_____

_____

_____

_____

_____

Day 16: It's All for Your Good

It was about 8 p.m., and past my two younger children's bedtime. As I was preparing my daughter for bed, she said: "Mommy, I'm hungry." I immediately thought about the time, in addition to the fact that I was tired.

"Okay, baby. You'll get breakfast in the morning," I responded quickly.

With some frustration and whining in her voice, she said, "Mommy, I am going to die. I'm so hungry!"

"You will be fine," I told her.

"No, Mommy! I am so hungry." Then I got "super spiritual" on my five-year-old. "Jesus went 40 days without eating and He didn't die."

"But He's more powerful than me!" she exclaimed.

I was in awe. Of course, I ended up feeding my baby before bed. Her pain and suffering ended with her gain—a full stomach!

Dear sister, "Jesus went 40 days without food."

Today is the day that I want you to realize that all you have gone through, and all you are going through in your career and your life, is not in vain. Jesus' life provides a powerful example of how suffering can work for our good. You're probably thinking like my daughter and saying, "But He is powerful!" Yes, He is; but Jesus was born a human and walked this life as man so that He could experience life as we do. It took His focus and discipline to stay true to His calling. Recognize that victory is already yours as a child of God. Everything that we go through is for our good. On the other side of this trial, you will be better. You will have more patience, more strength to endure and enhanced character.

In hindsight, when I look back on the times when I felt like I would die because of my suffering, I can't help but to remember 2017! During this trial at work, I used to think about the severity of the situation and how painful it was to go through. I cried at the drop of a dime whenever I thought of my situation. I walked down this long stretch sidewalk to my office one morning with a girlfriend who worked in a different line of business. As I shared examples of things that were happening to me with her, she was in awe. She felt my pain. The tears started to flow. She grabbed my shoulders to turn my body into a direction where people could not see. As she prayed for me, I was reminded of the sufferings of Jesus. Jesus suffered way more than I was suffering. If I could just focus on the promise like He did, I could make it. I knew trouble would not last always. I just had to get through "the going through" phase with my eyes fixed on Jesus.

Please be encouraged, knowing that the same power that Jesus used to stay focused on His mission lies within you. Redirect your thoughts and remember that, on the other side of pain and suffering, is the beauty of victory! God has already promised you that because of your mere acceptance of Jesus Christ, you have victory. Look up, my sister. It's all for your good.

In His pain and anguish, Jesus experienced a very human moment. He asked God to take the cup from Him. Have you ever asked God that? Jesus prefaced His request with, "If it be *your* will." Sometimes, we must endure the pain to reap the reward. Aren't you glad Jesus remained true to His promise so that we could live? He bore our sins (Luke 22:42; Isaiah 53).

Exercise

Can you think of a time when you had to relinquish your will and human desires to see *His* will through?

_____

_____

_____

_____

_____

_____

_____

_____

_____

Today, focus. Focus on the calling on your life; work as unto the Lord. Have self-control in your thoughts and feelings by reflecting on the life and death of Jesus.

Prayer

Dear God, today I choose to remember that my pain is not in vain. I choose to look for the good in this experience for my life. Help me to keep this in mind as I hold my head up. I am victorious. In Jesus' name. Amen.

Scriptures for Reflection

Romans 5:3-5; 8:28

Psalm 100:5

Meditation

Be still. Set your timer for 10 minutes. Hear God's voice as He reveals the lesson(s) in your current circumstances.

* * *

Journal your talk with God. What is He teaching you?

_____

_____

_____

_____

_____

_____

_____

_____

_____

_____

_____

_____

_____

_____

_____

_____

_____

_____

_____

Day 17: Guard Your Actions

When I received my first operations assignment, I was terrified. I wanted so badly to prove myself. I thought my boss took a "risk" appointing me into this position. Given my dominant, Type-A personality, my natural tendency is to get results! I will drive hard to get results. Sometimes, this can be to my detriment, especially when I feel threatened.

My direct reports didn't play well with me. They didn't think I was qualified for the job. They felt like I got the job because of who I knew, so they were bitter. To top that off, a new boss came in with a preconceived notion about me. He essentially told me that he wasn't sure I would make it and that maybe I needed to go back to a business role. As you could imagine, I felt pressured to show my boss I was capable to handle the position. This did not go over well with my team of direct reports.

As a result, I became selfish. My focus was me—my success, my performance. After all, I had to survive and get results. My reputation was on the line to prove that I could do this work. Wrong! As a leader, your focus should always be on others first, then self. The moment we focus on ourselves, we risk the chance of exhibiting toxic behaviors that only make our situations worse. In my situation, my dominant personality style was perceived as aggressive and a form of micromanagement. I was under pressure to maintain my top performance that I achieved throughout my career prior to that job.

Think about what pressures you are under and the motives behind your actions. Be mindful that you are acting in a way that demonstrates your commitment to the business first, the team second, and yourself last. Guard your actions—*not only* in your interactions with your family and friends—but in the secular arena, as well. Remember, at the end of the day, you shine for Christ.

Jesus coined servant leadership with His disciples. When they disputed over who was the greatest, He humbled them by telling them the one who serves is greatest among them. (Luke 22:24-27).

Exercise

You lead by example. People will choose to follow you by what you do. Jesus inspired His followers through His actions. What are your actions telling others?

_____

_____

_____

_____

_____

Prayer

God, thank you for this new day and for new perspectives. I want you to always shine brightly through me as I interact with colleagues, direct reports and those who are in leadership. Guard my actions today so that I represent you well. Help me keep my priorities in order so that I build trust. In Jesus' name. Amen.

Scriptures for Reflection

Romans 8:28

Psalm 1

John 16:33

Meditation

Set your timer for 10 minutes. Quiet your mind. Don't focus on yourself; just focus on Him. Listen to Him. Let Him guide you.

* * *

Journal your prayer time with the Lord. How is God helping you to lead effectively in the secular arena?

_____

_____

_____

_____

_____

_____

_____

_____

_____

_____

_____

_____

_____

_____

_____

_____

_____

_____

Day 18: Loved by Him

Oh, how I love Sundays! When my heart is aching, there's no other place I would rather be than in the house of the Lord. The sweet sounds of praise and worship music, the loving arms of fellow Christians, and the unadulterated Word of God proclaimed gives me life. One Sunday, I was aching so badly that I could hardly hold myself up. As we stood during praise and worship, I felt like I was in a daze. My body was physically there, but my mind was so captivated by the pain from a heart-wrenching situation.

I wished that either my girlfriend on my left, or my husband on my right, could somehow grab the suffering from me and throw it away. I felt my body slowly taking me down. I just laid my head in my folded arms on the seats in the row in front of us. I wanted and needed help so badly! Suddenly, I tuned into the lyrics of the song *Good, Good Father*. In that moment, I got what I needed!

I simply needed to be reminded of my Father, who loves me. As I considered the words and allowed them to minister to my soul, I was able to lift my head. Then, my body followed. I stood to my feet and lifted my hands in total praise and surrender to Him. I could not only feel His presence, but His love for me. I was reminded that, when you are loved, you are taken care of.

Today, my sister in Christ, I want to remind you of who you are! We have a good, good Father who loves us. We are never alone. When it feels unbearable and impossible to even breathe, remember that, because of His love, you win. Because of His love, we can experience an unexplainable peace. Because of His love, we can rest in the arms of the perfect one. Go in peace today, knowing who *you* are – loved by God.

Prayer

Thank you, God, for having such a deep love for me. Thank you for giving me peace and comfort. Thank you for being my good, good Father, perfect in every way. Help me to recall who I am in you every second of this day. When I get weary, remind me that your love means that you got me. Help me to hold my head high and proclaim your love to others around me. Let my life be a walking witness of love. In pure obedience, I surrender it all to you. I love you, God. Amen.

Exercise

One of the most memorable stories of people worshipping and dedicating their lives to God was Pentecost. The Holy Spirit rested on the people that day, and God's love shone on a great crowd that day (Acts 2).

How will you bask in your Father's love today?

_____

_____

_____

_____

Scriptures for Reflection

Isaiah 26:3-4

1 John 4:18

Song for Reflection

"Good, Good Father" by Chris Tomlin

Meditation

Set your timer for 10 minutes. Quiet your mind.

* * *

Take a moment to think about what you read today and write down what is coming up for you. How can you use this day's reading for your own situation?

_____

_____

_____

_____

_____

_____

_____

_____

_____

_____

_____

_____

_____

_____

_____

_____

_____

_____

Day 19: Loving Myself First

Why is it so hard for us to totally accept who we are?

It complicates everything in life when we aren't fully content with who we are. It shows up in our everyday dealings at work, with family and with friends. It's simply something that can't be hidden, even when we think we are masking our lack of self-love with a smile, with clothes, jewelry and other surface things. With the unsettled nature of our feelings toward ourselves, it doesn't take much to send us into a pit of comparison, lack and even pity. I believe we tend to be more defensive in nature when things happen, thinking they are happening *to us* versus happening *for us*. One of the keys to recovering from perceived failure is loving yourself through the process—loving yourself for every thought, every feeling, every desire and every action. I know this can be a challenge, especially when you feel you are the cause of a situation.

For as long as I can remember, I have always questioned myself, my decisions and my behavior. At one point, I would leave work each day, replaying scenarios from the day and getting upset with myself for responding the way I did. Things got so bad with the criticism that I would get stress headaches. The headaches were a result of me over-analyzing and critiquing each word I said, in addition to each action. This was not healthy. I knew that to be fully free to live out my potential, I had to give myself the space and the grace to be me: the perfectly imperfect me, the one who gives herself permission to not have it all together and try to look like I did. The Bible clearly tells us in Psalm 139:14 that we are fearfully and wonderfully made, and that the works of the Lord are marvelous. If this is the case, then why can't we love ourselves the way God created us? When we don't love who we are, we are literally calling God a liar. I don't believe any of us want to do that!

I was always one to encourage others and to let them know how great they are. But I didn't totally love me. Earlier in this book, I mentioned the challenge I offered to my Bible study group to write each day for 21 days. We had to write ten things we loved about ourselves. We had to check in with each other daily for accountability. After the 21 days, I kept going with the challenge until I felt healing from the "criticism sickness" I possessed. Finally, I learned how to love myself first. Doing this opened me up to loving others better and showing up in a more comfortable way.

Exercise

Your challenge today is to embrace every aspect of yourself and love it. You are gifted with talents that the world needs. Don't risk falling short; love yourself more. As you love yourself, you will have the love necessary to share with others more than you ever have.

Take a moment and list 10 things you love about yourself.

1. _____

2. _____

3. _____

4. _____

5. _____

6. _____

7. _____

8. _____

9. _____

10. _____

Prayer

God, thank you for making me who I am. Help me to reflect and to remember how much you love me. As I bask in your love, help me to love myself like you love me. Then God, teach me how to do what your Word says in I Corinthians 13, which is to love. I thank you for exemplifying the greatest form of love by giving your darling Son, Jesus Christ, for me. May I honor you with love and obedience. In Jesus' name. Amen.

Scriptures for Reflection

Psalm 139:14-16

I Corinthians 13

John 3:16

Meditation

Set your timer for 10 minutes. Quiet your mind.

* * *

Take a moment to think about what you read today and write down what is coming up for you. How can you use this day's reading for your own situation?

_____

_____

_____

_____

_____

_____

_____

_____

_____

_____

_____

_____

_____

_____

_____

_____

_____

_____

_____

_____

_____

_____

_____

_____

_____

_____

_____

PART III:

Moving On: Turn Your Mess into Your Message

Day 20: Focus on the Possibilities

My dear sister, how are you doing today? Really take a moment to consider how you are doing. If someone asked you today, "How are you doing?" what would you say?

By now, you probably have felt the move of God on your situation, and you're feeling a little lighter. You may have even seen His handiwork revealed in your life. Before I knew it, I felt some relief from a significantly impactful situation in my life. I was going into a place of work every day where I knew, without a shadow of a doubt, that I was only tolerated, not accepted. It was the worst, most unfulfilling place to be in ever! Yet, each day, I walked in with a smile and my head up, ready to do my part. Each day that I stepped onto the campus, I felt like I was getting closer to my release. I could see the light at the end of the tunnel, where God rescues me and sets me on the course of my new level. I knew that I was experiencing some deep character growth. It was building the fortitude necessary to take me higher in Him. Just the focus on the possibility of approaching my release kept me putting one foot in front of the other.

Today, reflect on the fact that God has your back and has already promised you victory. Recall the little things He has shown you through this situation and journal them. As you recall them, give God praise. There is triumph in the praise. Direct your attention to how you will be better on the other side of this trial. What things have you learned from this? How will those learnings make you better in the future? What are the possibilities for your career as a result of the growth? List the answers to these questions and think on these things today.

_____

_____

_____

_____

_____

_____

_____

_____

Now, I believe that your responses are positive since you have already been promised victory! It's time for you to walk into His victory as you stay focused on what's possible for you. I believe in you. God believes in you and your loved ones believe in you. Do *you* believe in *you*? Say, "Yes!" with confidence.

So, how are you doing today? Smile and be wonderful!

As an Israelite mother was hiding her son among the reeds in the Nile River to save him from execution, did she ever conceive that he would grow up to be the future prince of Egypt and later be called on by God as the savior of the Israelites? As Moses' mother sought to save the life of her son, she remained focused on the possibilities of what he could one day accomplish.

Prayer

Lord, I thank you for your daughter and the victory that already lies in front of her. Help her to know, without a doubt, that she is victorious. Therefore, God, she can focus on the possibilities versus the struggle. In Jesus' name. Amen.

Scriptures for Reflection

Exodus 2:1-4

Exodus 3

Exercise

What possibilities lie ahead for you?

_____

_____

_____

_____

Meditation

Set your timer for 15 minutes. Quiet your mind.

* * *

Take a moment to think about what you read today and write down what is coming up for you. How can you use this day's reading for your own situation?

_____

_____

_____

_____

_____

_____

_____

_____

_____

_____

_____

_____

Day 21: How You Respond

Rise and shine, my sister! Give God the glory for a new day and a new chance to do things differently. I had a chance to speak to a new leader on my team. She found herself in the midst of recovering from what could have been a critical mistake. When I saw her, she looked like her spirit was cast down. What she probably knew was that I had heard about the mistake, so she talked in a discouraged tone.

"I don't know why and how I did that. It was such a rookie mistake," she said. "I'm supposed to be a leader; they look to me for help. Look what I did."

"You are human," I said. "'We all eat, sleep and pass waste the same,'" as my mother would say. But what separates you as a leader is how you respond to the experience of defeat or failure."

My sister, perhaps you have been feeling dismayed and discouraged from your failure, defeat or shame. But I want to encourage you to consider what you will do with this. How will you make lemonade out of lemons?

"What can you do to learn and teach others from this mistake such that we keep others from doing the same thing?" I asked her. She began to think and brainstorm. The story condensed. She decided to "fess up" to her team and admit her failure. She decided to tell the impact on self, the team and the business. She shared what could be done differently to avoid this mistake in the future and asked for all to be accountable to one another. She left this conversation feeling encouraged and inspired. It's not what happens to you that determines who you are, it's how you respond to what happens to you. It is in the thick of the intensity of the struggle that one truly sees who they are and what they are made of. How are you responding? Let's rise and shine.

As I reflect on today's reading, I think about those in the Bible who made mistakes. Yet, their mistakes were not the end of them or their fate in life. They were still used by God to do His work.

Exercise

Take some time today to study the following people in the Bible and answer the following questions: How did they respond to their situation? How did God respond and what is the message from their life? Where do you need to respond differently to your own situation with grace today?

Noah

_____

_____

_____

_____

_____

_____

Moses

_____

_____

_____

_____

_____

_____

King David

_____

_____

_____

_____

_____

Jonah

_____

_____

_____

_____

_____

Peter

_____

_____

_____

_____

_____

_____

Prayer

God, thank you for teaching me a valuable lesson on how to respond to trials of many kinds. Help me to honor you and be true to myself in my response. Help me to rise and shine as a true leader. May you always get the glory out of my life. May your joy reside within me so that others see you, and only you, when they look at me. Amen.

Scriptures for Reflection

Romans 12:17-19

Romans 13:14

Meditation

Set your timer for 15 minutes. Quiet your mind.

* * *

Take a moment to think about what you read today and write down what is coming up for you. How can you use this day's reading for your own situation?

_____

_____

_____

_____

_____

_____

_____

_____

Day 22: Back to Basics

Alright, sister. Life hit us hard, and we completely lost ourselves! So much so that it was extremely difficult to face the giants in our lives. But God wastes nothing! He uses everything for our good to build the depth of our character, which is necessary to go to the next level. Out of the deepest pain one could ever feel was the birth of the B.O.L.D. Factor™ system.

You see, I had to figure out some way to step outside of feeling like a total failure. I needed to transition quickly because, as a solution-focused person, I could not stay where I was too long. I needed to own what I could and use my experience to catapult me to the next level in my life and career.

Because I owned the situation, I was able to raise my energy level from victim mode. I was also able to realize another aspect of the calling on my life...*you!* Yes, you, my sister. You see, God told me 14 years prior to my darkest time that the call on my life was to impact women all over the world so they would overcome obstacles in a way that elevates them into success. I didn't know how that could possibly happen, as I didn't know much about anything that would transform *people...women...anybody.*

Then, 14 years later, B.O.L.D. Factor™ came for you and me. I want to share this concept with you so that you can own your B.O.L.D. Factor™ and move on with your life in a more powerful way. Let's begin!

B is for Back to Basics. Many people take this step for granted. They often see it as too "touchy feely" with no direct results that affect the bottom line. It wasn't until I did the introspective work necessary that I regained myself again, but in a deeper way. I uncovered my "why" and shifted to that focus.

My "why":

- To use my life experiences to teach and inspire others so that they overcome obstacles keeping them from their next level of impact.

- I believe people have what they need inside of them to lead in life, work and community. All experiences—good and bad—build the depth and character necessary to go to the next level.

- My life has been filled with hard challenges; yet, I take the impossible and make it possible through Christ!

- My desire is to see people play full out in life, work and community so they can experience vitality in life. They won't be worried about discrimination, exclusion or rejection. I want to see them use tough experiences to advance in life, work and community. I believe we were created by the most powerful, majestic, high God, who didn't mess up when He made us. He wants all His children to walk in this authority so that we make ultimate impact for His glory!

Shifting my focus and operating on purpose made me work differently. It allowed me to make a more positive impact. To this day, I have people who watched me go through tough times of my life and have said how much I have inspired them. One lady said the only reason she stayed in her job with our company is because of me. Wow!

Let me give credit where credit is due. It was actually my husband who first read Simon Sinek's book, *Finding Your Why,* which led me through the process of finding my "why." The process of finding it took weeks! Every time I thought I had figured it out, I shared it with him. He'd ask, "Why?" After several iterations of answering the one-word question, I finally found it! You can, too! Get clear on your purpose and use that as the lens through which you make decisions.

O is for Own Your Own Strengths. Every successful person I know is crystal clear on what they are good at. What makes them successful is owning and operating in their strengths. Therefore, learn to embrace and operate in your strengths.

I was so focused on not disappointing my boss or mentors that I forgot how to just be me and how to operate in what I do best. In fact, my confidence was so damaged. I gave too much power to my inner critic. Do more of what you are good at. We will discuss what the L and D of the B.O.L.D. Factor™ means as we move forward.

Prayer

Dear God, thank you for equipping me with everything I need to lead in life, work and my community. Help me to clearly define my purpose and discover my strengths, so I can play full out as you have called me to do. I incline my ear to you today and every day. Amen.

Exercise

What is your why? What is the thing that moves you and drives you into action when you think about it? What's the thing that gives you a sense of urgency to do more of?

_____

_____

_____

_____

_____

_____

_____

_____

What are your strengths? What are you good at? What things come naturally to you? How will you use them to make more impact?

_____

_____

_____

_____

_____

_____

_____

_____

_____

_____

_____

_____

Scriptures for Reflection

Luke 6:38

1 Corinthians 12

Meditation

Set your timer for 15 minutes. Quiet your mind.

* * *

Take a moment to think about what you read today and write down what is coming up for you. How can you use this day's reading for your own situation?

_____

_____

_____

_____

_____

_____

_____

_____

_____

_____

_____

_____

_____

_____

_____

_____

_____

_____

Day 23: Victory Is Yours, So Lead

As a leader, you make the first move. I didn't know what this meant until I found myself in a situation of conspiracy where false accusations were lodged against me. I knew the source of the accusations and had to work with them on a frequent basis, as if nothing happened. They may not know that I knew they were the source, but it didn't matter. For me to lead with integrity and freedom, I had to *recover* fast and move on. I had to go first, which means I had to forgive first. I had to move on, treat everyone fairly, and take care of each person in my organization. After all, I was the leader.

I can't tell you this was easy, but it wasn't hard. With God's help, I was able to own the situation, the time, and what I needed to do to be a better person and leader. As I did this, I took my attention and eyes off others. It became increasingly easy as I looked to the good that would come from the situation. Once again, I placed my focus on the victory instead of the people. When you have your eyes on victory, you don't have to wish, want or worry; just praise Him. Now, let's finish the B.O.L.D. Factor™ from yesterday.

L – Listen More, Talk Less. Leaders are to listen to perspectives and consider others' points of view before speaking to show that they care about others. This requires the leader to use extreme control to keep their opinions on hold until everyone else is heard. As leaders, we often think we need to put our voice into the room so that others know that we have answers. Yet, instead, if you must speak, let it be to ask questions to gain clarity on the perspectives in the room. Our time will come in which we must speak. Use discernment.

D - Don't Be Afraid of Feedback. This pertains to both giving and receiving feedback from those around you. Feedback is a gift; it allows growth and fosters a transparent environment for making real change. The hard thing about feedback is the initial perception is that it's bad news. Feedback is for encouragement, recognition and equipping. It should be given and received in a collaborative, not condemning way. Keep this in mind for peers, leaders, direct reports, family, and friends. Without feedback, we cannot live in an authentic and victorious way.

Pray for God's enlightenment, wisdom and guidance relative to your B.O.L.D. Factor™. Get the help you need and keep pressing. It would be my pleasure to help you with this. Contact me today.

Today, clear your mind and redirect yourself to victory. Capture the essence of the hope you feel when you can look ahead, lead first, forgive, let go and let God. You are expected to be this kind of leader. People are counting on you to be this kind of leader. Don't wait for the battle to be over; shout now! Hallelujah!

Prayer

Lord, thank you for a victorious end! Thank you for giving me a new, fresh focus. Keep me looking ahead. Clear my path so I can walk on. May this situation touch the lives of others in a positive way as they witness how I go through. Help me to own my B.O.L.D. Factor™. In Jesus' name. Amen.

Exercise

What has recently happened to you that you initially took offensively? If you take a step back and listen to what was said, could you understand the other person's perspective?

_____

_____

_____

What is one difficult conversation that you need to have with someone?

_____

_____

_____

What is the specific thing that happened?

_____

_____

_____

What impact did it have on you?

_____

_____

_____

_____

What would you like to see differently in the future?

_____

_____

_____

_____

Now take this as preparation and have your conversation!

Scriptures for Reflection

Romans 5:3-5

Meditation

Set your timer for 15 minutes. Quiet your mind.

* * *

Take a moment to think about what you read today and write down what is coming up for you. How can you use this day's reading for your own situation?

_____

_____

_____

_____

_____

_____

_____

_____

_____

_____

_____

_____

_____

_____

_____

_____

_____

_____

Day 24: Own Your Strengths

Today, lets build upon one of the concepts of the B.O.L.D. Factor™. Think about what you are good at. What are your strengths? When you are feeling great, making progress, contributing to the fullest and impacting those around you in a positive way, what are you doing?

Experiencing a highly visible failure in my career made me second guess myself, my knowledge, abilities and skills. To hear someone tell you that they had not heard anything good about you in the less than one-year tenure with the company was more than disheartening. I managed to build myself back up from that blow. Then, to hear someone tell you that "you will never be another line leader on this site" left me feeling angry! How could this happen to me?

Moving from anger to victim was an easy transition. When your thinking is stinking, you show up that way. Somehow, some way, I had to figure out how to stay focused on what I do know. Without a doubt, I know who I am and whose I am. I am equipped with everything needed to lead. I made a non-negotiable decision to own my strengths and to do more of them. As I rebuilt, the paradigm totally shifted from less of a fight to more of a collaboration. When you are operating in your strengths, you operate in excellence. Excellence is an attractive magnet that draws people in to you. When you own and operate in your strengths, it fuels your passion. Passion flows from your heart and touches the heart of others. Passion builds momentum and facilitates an environment where others seek you out for your opinion and expertise. Nobody can do what you do like you do it, so own your strengths!

What about you? Are you owning your strengths and doing more of what comes naturally? What are your strengths outlined in the prior chapter? I challenge you to own them and play full out!

Prayer

God, you have equipped me with unique gifts, talents and strengths that only I possess and can fulfill. Help me to embrace them and play full out. Let me not look to my left or to my right, but to press forward to fulfilling my destiny as you have designed. Open doors and opportunities for me to walk into boldly. May my gifts make room for me and may you be the only standard I work toward. Amen.

Exercise

Are you embodying the strengths God gave you?

_____

_____

_____

What opportunities are waiting for you to walk into where you can use your God-given strengths?

_____

_____

_____

_____

_____

What commitment will you make today?

_____

_____

_____

_____

_____

_____

_____

_____

_____

Who will hold you accountable for walking out your purpose?

_____

_____

_____

_____

_____

Scriptures for Reflection

Colossians 3:17, 22-24

Meditation

Set your timer for 15 minutes. Quiet your mind.

* * *

Take a moment to think about what you read today and write down what is coming up for you. How can you use this day's reading for your own situation?

_____

_____

_____

_____

_____

_____

_____

_____

_____

_____

_____

_____

_____

_____

_____

_____

_____

_____

_____

Day 25: Seat at the Table

It amazes me when I see people walk into the conference room for a meeting. They see open chairs at the table, yet they choose to sit in a seat against the wall or in the back of the room. It almost immediately sends a subliminal message of insecurity and feeling "less than." There were times when I just wanted to play small and stay lowkey. I wanted to choose a seat against the wall or at the back of the room. Those times were deep and dark for me. In fact, I felt like I walked around with a sign on my forehead that read, "Failure."

In these moments, it took a lot of self-talk and prayer to push beyond my insecurities and choose the open seat at the table. You are a leader. Leaders lead in season and out of season, in good times and bad times. God didn't make us to be lowkey. Instead, He equipped us to engage, to be the head and not the tail. God has equipped us to be first and not last. He equipped us to be wonderful, to let our light shine, and to work as unto Him. Being a leader means leading followers. True leadership is about serving those who we work with.

How can you play small when those you serve are counting on you to pave the way? They are counting on us to get knowledge and experiences, then pass on the lessons. We are called to be women of power and influence. This means that we are a part of God's story and design. As God's design, He is for us and has given us the authority to be under His authority! We are pioneers, mentors and coaches. Let's turn our mess into our message, get vulnerable and lead others.

No matter what is going on in your head today, push through. Remember who you are and take your seat at the table. Be a great example and role model for others to follow. Be the King's daughter. Hold your prominent position in the land of the living. Lead, sister! Lead!

Prayer

Heavenly Father, thank you for giving me a seat at the table as a leader in this land. In my times of deepest despair, help me to remember the royalty that has been given to me as your daughter. Help me to leverage the power of the team and to focus on leading, empowering and developing others. Even though I may have a seat at the table, may I only open my mouth whenever you prompt me to. May I consider the business and team first. Give me a sense of urgency to be about your business! In Jesus' Name. Amen.

Exercise

One of the most admirable women of the Bible, and as I mentioned before my favorite, was Deborah. Deborah was a middle-aged prophet, who was highlighted in Judges 4 and 5, who had an anointing on her life to lead the Israelites in the battle against the Canaanites. How she went about doing this was impressive. Check out her story and record her leadership style here.

What did you notice about how she responded to God's call?

_____

_____

_____

_____

_____

_____

What big projects are you called to in which you're feeling inadequate?

_____

_____

_____

_____

_____

What lessons can you glean from Deborah's story to help you move into action?

_____

_____

_____

_____

_____

Scriptures for Reflection:

Judges 4 & 5

Ephesians 2:8

Ecclesiastes 3:1

Meditation

Set your timer for 15 minutes. Quiet your mind.

* * *

Take a moment to think about what you read today and write down what is coming up for you. How can you use this day's reading for your own situation?

_____

_____

_____

_____

_____

_____

_____

_____

_____

_____

_____

_____

_____

_____

_____

_____

_____

_____

_____

Day 26: Walk in Boldness

Oh, how sweet it is to be able to walk in pure boldness as a child of the Most High God! As Christians, we have rights like no other humans on the face of the earth! We have been bought with a redemptive price! No matter how crazy, sad, unfair or detrimental things may appear, we can walk peacefully through those times because we have been chosen by God!

I was out doing my leadership line walk one day when I stopped to talk with one of the employees. Fifteen minutes into the conversation, she said, "You know people are wondering how you are still standing, right?" In that moment, my heart leaped for joy for a couple of reasons:

1. It was a prime time for God to get glory through a verbal testimony.

2. There was recognition of my press amid the storm, which in turn, encouraged others.

I smiled at her and thought about what I could say that wouldn't prompt a hotline call to Human Resources for religion in the workplace! I simply responded, "My faith is what has kept me and has allowed me to stand, even when I didn't feel like it."

What I really wanted to say is, "I'm a kept daughter of the Most High

God and, because of the price His darling Son paid on the cross for me, I can walk boldly through any and every situation with faith. I know who God is, and He promised me that I am already victorious!" Yes, that's what I *really* wanted to say. But as leaders in corporate America, we must use wisdom. We must choose our words carefully. More than anything, we must walk out our faith so that others know!

Today, walk boldly through the hallways of your workplace. Walk like you know who you are. Even if you don't feel it, walk like it anyway! Hold your head up, put a smile on your face, and be a King's kid! You never have to wait until the battle is over. You can shout right now! Jehovah Nissi is our banner of victory. Call Him today and own your B.O.L.D. Factor™!

Prayer

Father, I'm so blessed to walk with my head held high in pure boldness because of your promises. I am thankful for your word and promises. I am honored and humbled that I can come directly to you with all of me and you will comfort me. Thank you for being so far ahead of me that you have every situation worked out. I appreciate being able to be your instrument. May you get the glory this day. In Jesus' name. Amen!

Scriptures for Reflection

Romans 8:1

Hebrews 4:16

I Peter 5:6

Joshua 1:5-9

Meditation

Set your timer for 15 minutes. Quiet your mind.

* * *

Take a moment to think about what you read today and write down what is coming up for you. How can you use this day's reading for your own situation?

_____

_____

_____

_____

_____

_____

_____

_____

_____

_____

_____

_____

_____

_____

_____

_____

_____

_____

Day 27: Fess Up and Get Help

People are constantly watching us. Our actions and behaviors set the tone for the organization. We are expected to show up with positivity, vision and support. After a failure, people will watch to see how you'll allow the experience to affect you. They are looking to see if you will retaliate, defend, deflect or reflect.

One time, I had a situation that I felt would ultimately be the end of my career! I was embarrassed and ashamed to face my family. But after counsel, I was able to make a conscious choice to reflect by looking at the themes of behaviors that caused my leadership to derail. As I reflected, I knew I could not turn the situation around by myself. I needed help from my team. I confessed to them with transparency and authenticity, then I asked if they would help me turn things around. I needed them to become advocates for me. They agreed to help, and this was the best thing I could have done. The entire organization was watching and waiting to see what I would do. I later learned that many saw the transition and change in my approach and, as a result, they respected me for it.

What are you going to do? How will you show up? What story will you create from your experience? Choose to reflect, fess up, get help and make a change in you. You are the only one who can control *you*.

Prayer

Lord, I know all eyes are on me as a leader. Please don't let me hinder the organization from moving forward. Help me to reflect, fess up, get help and change for the better. May the people around me have the grace that I need to move on. May the people around me be blessed by what they've witnessed through me. May others learn of the process for restoration through what they have seen me do. Thank you for the victory. In Jesus' name. Amen.

Exercise

Are you moving or allowing the past to dictate your future?

_____

_____

_____

_____

What old news do you need to let go of?

_____

_____

_____

_____

How will you proceed as a result of today's reading?

_____

_____

_____

_____

Scriptures for Reflection

Philippians 3:14

Ephesians 2:10

Meditation

Set your timer for 15 minutes. Quiet your mind.

* * *

Take a moment to think about what you read today and write down what is coming up for you. How can you use this day's reading for your own situation?

_____

_____

_____

_____

_____

_____

_____

_____

_____

_____

_____

_____

_____

_____

_____

_____

_____

_____

Day 28: Keep God on Your Mind

This is the day the Lord has made. Let us rejoice and be glad in it. Rejoice in the Lord. Again, I say, rejoice! Praise His name from whom all blessings flow. What a mighty God we serve! Who can come between God and us? No one.

Each morning, I read my devotional before I read anything else. No email, text messages or social media come before first planting God's Word in my heart. I find this is a critical part of my day. I noticed that, when I read other things first, I was distracted. My mind was all over the place. I started trying to answer emails, solve problems, compare things and myself, which led to me getting off focus for the day. Yet, when I decided to start my morning with God, and I stayed true to that over the past five and half years, I am reminded of God throughout the day.

Once I get my Word in for the day, while I am getting dressed, I play my gospel music and sing! Singing and giving God praise takes my mind off me and my mess, and places it on our mighty God. When praises go up, blessings come down. When we praise, we shut Satan out. He cannot stay in the same place as our praise; it's like a stinky smell to his nostrils! So, I let him have it first thing in the morning.

During my ride to work in the morning, I put on a sermon, podcast or audio book to continually feed my mind with positivity. As leaders, we should continue to develop ourselves by filling our minds with knowledge. Constantly meditating and thinking of positive things, gives us life and fuel.

Some mornings, I choose to talk on the phone to one of my sisters so we can encourage and sharpen one another.

All these things—devotion, praise, listening and talking positively—prepare me for whatever I may face throughout the day. Sometimes, throughout the day, I need a refresh of praise. It's not uncommon to catch me walking the halls with a song from my lips. This is what helps me make it through! How about you? I encourage you to burst into this day with God on your mind and keep Him there all day. As you keep Him there, listen for downloads into your spirit. Listen for what moves to make, what people to engage, and what stories to share. Keep Him on your mind.

Prayer

Father, thank you for a new day, new mercies and new opportunities to be used by you. Help me to remember the words that are being spoken in my ear. May I meditate on your word throughout this day. In Jesus' name. Amen.

Exercise

What podcast, book or personal development will you commit to today?

_____

_____

Who will you ask to join you?

_____

_____

Scriptures for Reflection

Psalm 100

1 Thessalonians 5:23

Meditation

Set your timer for 15 minutes. Quiet your mind.

* * *

Take a moment to think about what you read today and write down what is coming up for you. How can you use this day's reading for your own situation?

_____

_____

_____

_____

_____

_____

_____

_____

_____

_____

_____

_____

_____

_____

_____

_____

_____

_____

Day 29: Your Advisory Board Matters

Today is "take action day!" That's right, my sister! It's time for you to build your advisory board or reconnect with your existing board. Who do you have on your side to encourage you, share with you, mentor you and vouch for you? Who are your advocates when discussions are taking place behind closed doors? Who are your safe places?

An advisory board, in this context, is the team of people who provide advice in an informal or formal nature to you. I like to have someone:

1. Who is higher up than I am and who has the authority to make decisions or influence decisions about me.

2. Who is a mentor who has been there, done that, and is where I'm going and can share best practices.

3. Who is a peer and someone who will give me honest feedback and complement me where I may be weak.

4. Who I can share personal things with and know that they will tell me the real deal.

5. Who can coach me to find the answers from within. They don't need to know the answers. But they know what questions to ask me to pull the answers out.

One time, I had a situation when I didn't know what else to do to help get through it. Because I was fearful of the potential negative impact on my career, I didn't call anyone for help. I just dealt with it. But then, things got so unbearable that I realized I needed a lifeline! I rationalized with myself that, surely, all the progressive leaders I knew must have fallen on hard times before in order to make it to where they were.

I finally talked myself into reaching out to three people in my network or advisory board. One person I looked at as my sponsor. One was a friend/mentor, and the other was a new mentor. From this experience, I realized who really had my back. Two out of three were huge contributors to helping me overcome my struggle. This was a great example of not only the importance of having an advisory board, but also using it! It is so important to stay connected, have regular contacts, and let them know what you're up to. I firmly believe that you must have an advisory board at your disposal. Reach out sooner than later when you're in need.

One final member for your advisory board outside of the five (5) listed above, is a Therapist. You need a trained professional skilled at helping you understand your past and how it impacts you today. This person can also help you navigate through the struggles you may face in your life today. There is a stigma around having a therapist that I believe must be removed. They are a valuable resource for confidential sharing and unbias perspectives. Not to mention, their expertise is crucial in times of mental health concerns. Don't be afraid to reach out for the support you need.

Who's on your team? Today, take the action to build your team, schedule some one-on-one time, and let them know how you are doing.

Prayer

God, show me the people who are for me. Give them a heart for me and give me the courage to reach out to them. May they receive me with love and openness. Help me to listen and understand. Give me discernment in all things. May the relationships blossom organically, as you would have them to. Open the doors of opportunity for me to serve on the advisory board of others who are coming along behind me. May I be a benefit to them and provide the guidance needed for their success. In Jesus' name. Amen.

Exercise

Name at least five people you would like to have on your advisory board and why.

1. _____
2. _____
3. _____
4. _____
5. _____

What do you have to offer them?

_____

_____

_____

_____

Who would you like to mentor?

_____

_____

_____

_____

When will you contact each person?

_____

_____

_____

_____

Scriptures for Reflection

Titus 2:1-5

James 1:22-25

Proverbs 27:17

Meditation

Set your timer for 15 minutes. Quiet your mind.

* * *

Take a moment to think about what you read today and write down what is coming up for you. How can you use this day's reading for your own situation?

_____

_____

_____

_____

_____

_____

_____

_____

_____

_____

_____

_____

_____

_____

Day 30: Failure is Okay

By now, I hope you realize that it's okay to have failures. It's okay to make mistakes. When we fail, we all face feelings of lost hope and feel like we can't be used. However, we know that in these times, we draw strength from God's Word and His promises. None of us are perfect on this earth. We all stumble; it's a part of life. Matter of fact, if you aren't having failures or making mistakes, you aren't really playing full out. You aren't really taking risks, making decisions and trying new things. I'm bold enough to say that you aren't growing either!

It took me a while to realize that I'm not some problem child or person who's the only one who messes up. I'm not the only one who experiences deep hurt. One time, I called someone after a tough fall, and they pretty much told me to just give up because I would never recover. They said, "just go do something else."

I left that conversation, feeling lower than dirt. I felt like the person just gave up on me. That person acted like someone who never experienced failure in their life. After much prayer and counsel from those who gave me grace, I realized that I wasn't the only one to experience such a low. So, I stopped by to tell you that God has the final say.

I stayed and turned things around. I refused to run away from my life lessons. If I had not stayed, I would not have the lessons and testimonies to share with you right now. Failure is the stop sign on the journey to success. Sometimes, we need to be stopped for the purpose to be fulfilled in the future. Sometimes, we must be stopped to get a lesson that matures us. If we get the lesson, we can move on. If we don't get the lesson, we must stay there! Don't miss the lesson! Get yourself moving, sis! Enjoy the journey in the process. Make this a great day.

Prayer

Thank you, God, for the trials, the failures and mistakes. I want to learn every lesson you have for me so I can move on. I don't want to stay in a place of, "Woe is me!" Instead, let me see my failure as a part of the journey to my success. I'm thankful that there is no failure in you! I'm thankful for the growth that you have already done in me. May you continue to do your perfect work in me. Amen.

Exercise

What lessons have you learned recently that you need to be reminded of, or that you need to keep practicing in order to advance yourself?

_____

_____

_____

_____

_____

_____

_____

Scriptures for Reflection

Romans 8:28

Philippians 1:6

Meditation

Set your timer for 15 minutes. Quiet your mind.

* * *

Take a moment to think about what you read today and write down what is coming up for you. How can you use this day's reading for your own situation?

_____

_____

_____

_____

_____

_____

_____

_____

_____

_____

_____

_____

_____

_____

_____

_____

_____

_____

_____

_____

Day 31: Heal Openly

It felt like I was the only one to ever experience the depth of hurt and pain I felt during that time. Not seeing anyone around me go through such, or at least share with me what they were going through, led me to believe that something was wrong with me. Little did I know that, as I began to share with others, so many people could relate to my experiences. What was even more astonishing is that as I shared openly, I healed faster!

Initially, sharing the most recent debacle in my life brought me to tears every time I talked about it. Yet, as I continued my journey to restoration, I noticed that every time I shared, God revealed a truth and a lesson. Each time a truth and lesson were revealed, the wound of my hurt closed even more. I incorporated the lessons in the story after the reveal, and this gave life and hope to those who listened. This helped others see that they, too, can keep it moving in the face of trials.

Trials come to make us stronger and wiser. They groom us for the season that we are entering. When we begin to see the seasons that we are in, we can handle the season in the right way. The things that hurt us and bring us pain are the very things designed to bring change. As we heal openly, God identifies and clarifies the call He has on our lives. Thus, turning our mess into His message!

Many people face trials and tribulations, then lose all hope for any possible good coming out of the situation. It almost feels like their plans and dreams are dying right before their eyes. Oftentimes, they can't feel the hand of the Lord upon them. Then, here comes *you*—the one who has new insights and vision, resolve in your heart, and clarity on the future for them! Jeremiah 29:11 assures us that God has plans to prosper us, not to harm us. This is the message you can have as you share your story openly. As you share, they heal. As they heal, you heal. Keep the domino effect going!

Exercise

What testimony do you have to share with others today? What is God prompting you to say and to who? Be on the lookout for opportunities to share with others. You will be surprised at how God uses your situation to bring hope and life to those you encounter.

_____

_____

_____

_____

_____

_____

_____

Prayer

God, open my eyes to opportunities to testify on your behalf. Prompt my spirit when you want me to share. Give me the words to say as you hide me behind the cross so you can come through. I don't want to do anything without your guidance. I will walk unhurriedly this day as I wait for you to use me in every way. I am your vessel, your instrument in this life on earth. As I share, continue to heal my heart so that I stand boldly in your name. Amen.

Scriptures for Reflection

Jeremiah 29:11

Amos 3:7

Meditation

Set your timer for 15 minutes. Quiet your mind.

* * *

Take a moment to think about what you read today and write down what is coming up for you. How can you use this day's reading for your own situation?

_____
_____
_____
_____
_____
_____
_____
_____
_____
_____
_____
_____
_____
_____
_____
_____
_____
_____

The Afterglow

God wants the very best for you. Jesus came that you might have life and have it more abundantly. God is not mad or punishing you; Jesus took on your punishment. Trials are meant to make you soar. *But they that wait upon the Lord shall renew their strength; they shall mount up with wings as eagles; they shall run, and not be weary; and they shall walk, and not faint* (Isaiah 40:31, KJV). Wait on God in His presence.

He who dwells in the secret place of the Most High Shall abide under the shadow of the Almighty (Psalm 91:1, NKJV).

He wants your life to count. *We are His workmanship, created in Christ Jesus for good works, which God prepared beforehand that we should walk in them* (Ephesians 2:10, NKJV). He wants you to leave impact and a legacy for generations to come.

Therefore, we do not lose heart. Even though our outward man is perishing, yet the inward man is being renewed day by day. For our light affliction, which is but for a moment, is working for us a far more exceeding and eternal weight of glory, while we do not look at the things which are seen, but at the things which are not seen. For the things which are seen are temporary, but the things which are not seen are eternal (2 Corinthians 4:16-18, NKJV).

Appendix A: Words Given to Me from the Mountains of Virginia

I'm so in awe of God. He amazes me how He orchestrates everything. He wastes nothing. Oh, how He loves on His children. How He meets every need.

I had the indescribable opportunity to sit at the feet of Jesus, my daddy, for five days in the mountains of Virginia—*alone*—in August of 2018. He knew I had hit rock bottom and was spiraling into the depths of depression. He knew my heart ached so badly from the hurt I experienced over these past three years. He knew I was burdened by the pain and shame I've carried throughout my life and could no longer hold it.

Let me tell you how much He loves *me (and He loves you, too)*. The opportunity presented itself for me to have some time alone. During this time, He enabled me to take a break from the chaos of life to remind me of who I am and whose I am. He reminded me that I'm more than enough and that my existence isn't an accident. He reminded me that I'm fearfully and wonderfully made. He reminded me that my failures aren't really failures. He reminded me that I am the head and not the tail.

He reminded me that no weapon formed against me shall prosper. He reminded me that He who began a good work in me shall complete it. He reminded me of the call on my life. He reminded me of the divine order:

wife, mother and everyone else. He reminded me that the women of the world need my testimony. He reminded me that in the struggle is where depth of character is given. He reminded me that my life story—the good, the bad, the ugly and the shame are for His people.

He reminded me that I am an open book that others need to read. He reminded me that I don't have to apologize for my different perspective, my direct nature, my desire to do things with excellence, and my outgoing personality. He reminded me of how amazing I am, how equipped I am, and how powerful I am through Him.

God challenged me to get out of the way and let Him do His thing. He challenged me to go boldly in God-confidence. He challenged me to let go—let go of the weeds of my past that have been suffocating the fruits of my garden. I let go and let God use me for His glory. I'm better and I'm ready, a vessel for God to use.

If you are struggling, I encourage you to rest in Him. Take time to get away from the familiar and let Daddy talk and love on you. Prayer is a conversation with God. Be quiet and let God talk to you while you listen. Then, get to work.

* * *

Here's what He specifically spoke to me:

> *My dear, sweet daughter, why are you so cast down, so overcome by hurt and withdrawn from the joy I so desire for you?*
>
> *Why is your heart leaking the sounds of pain and your voice trembling with grief?*
>
> *Why is your spirit so broken into itty bitty pieces and your dreams deferred?*
>
> *Why is there such a strong aroma of not being good enough, not being worthy, or being capable of handling the call that I have placed on your life?*

Why are you so fearful to step into the life that has been destined for you by the almighty God of the universe?

Why have you become so distant from who you are and whose you are?

Why have you forsaken your relevancy in the world, the calling on your life, the gifts you've been infiltrated with, the strengths that only you possess within?

Have I not told you over and over that you are fearfully and wonderfully made? That you are the head and not the tail? That I will be with you wherever you go? No weapon formed against you shall ever prosper. I have equipped you to thrive, drive and fly in this earthly world, where I once walked in human form so that I could feel what you feel.

My daughter, where is your faith and where is your belief in me? What happened that you lost touch, even after I gave you the vision? You wrote it with clarity and began to run...but... as you began to run and run so swiftly, that evil devourer knocked you down so hard that it took you off your feet. It has taken you so much longer to get up than ever before?

(Silently) I know that as you were down, he took the time to destroy you further by placing his right heel in your back. With the left one, he raised to drop it down on to your neck. But, don't you realize that I stopped him? I am who I am. I am the Great I Am. I am greater than he.

I am the Most High God, the most powerful force in the universe. Okay, baby. I know. I know you still feel the sting of his weight in the small of your back. I know it takes time to heal and you still have some crying to let out of your belly. I know. Shhhh. I am here for you. Daddy is here. As I lift you up in the air, twirl you around, and as I whisper in your ear, I want you to listen to me.

I want to remind you of some important things you have lost along the way. I want to remind you of your greatness and your beauty within. I want to remind you of the very elements I placed deep within your body, mind and soul. I want to remind you that I am the beginning and the end, that I am the Alpha and Omega. I am the first and last. Also, I am the one who began a good work within you and will complete it. I want to remind you, sweetheart, that I am the life giver, not you. When I remind you of all these things, please don't ever consider killing yourself again. Don't you ever consider taking your own life. That hurts me. Remember when you tried to take your life in the eleventh grade and I said, "No." I said, "Not yet." I said, "I have work for her to do." Even though you took every prescription pill you could find in that medicine cabinet, I did not take you out of here. You woke up the next day with your pastor by your side, saying, "It is not finished, my child." You have no control and authority over when your life is to end. When I am done with you, I will say, "Well done, thy good and faithful servant."

So, listen closely, my sweet. I have called you to impact women all over the world with your testimony of struggle, grace and mercy. You are called to tell your story—the good, the bad, the ugly and the embarrassing. You see, what Satan meant for your bad, I meant it for good. You are called to transform lives in a way that they will never return to the way they were before they encountered you. I have called you to use your uniqueness, your different perspective and outgoing personality to pave the way for others in life. You are not an accident, baby. I know that is contrary to what you have believed all these years...not having your biological father, not being truly accepted by those you meet, not feeling the love you so strongly desire. Forget those thoughts.

Let go. They are just sneaky little tricks of the enemy trying to steal, kill and destroy. He's trying to hold you back from being all that you can be at work, in business, as a wife, as a mother and as a friend. It places a veil, a barrier, an obstacle in the way. Then, it causes people to second guess you. They can't put their hands on it, but it's something there that keeps them from truly seeing the value you bring to life. Take down the veil. Take down the smokescreen and be your authentic self. Stop apologizing for your direct nature, your desire to follow the rules, your desire to get the work done with excellence first, then celebrate. Stop letting people make you think those things aren't good and that you are worthless because you don't know what they know. They don't know what you know, baby.

It's their own stuff that they are putting on you to kill your spirit, to slow your grind, to steal your joy, to stop your impact so that they feel better. So that they feel less intimidated. Enough is enough. You have work to do. You have lives to save. You have stories to tell. You have failures to share. By the way, those failures weren't really failures. They were lessons to build character, perseverance, faith and hope. They were story makers and placed upon you as testimonies of how good I am to my people. You are a transparent, open book. There are no skeletons in the closet.

Use every hurt, every trial, every failure, every situation, everything for my glory. You are enough; in fact, you are more than enough. You have everything you need to be all that you were placed on this earth to be. From now on, cast the enemy down. Flee from him. Shut him down with all your might. I will be right with you. Speak my Word in season and out of season. Rest each day in me. Meditate on my promises, day in and day out. Be intentional about your day and your time. Make choices that will serve your house first and the people second. Your first order of business is your husband. Respect him as your husband. Build him up and make him feel good. You are the only one in his life to do that. No one else can. I took his rib and gave it to you. He needs you to survive. If you are broken and disrespectful, how can you complete him? Your next order of business is your children. You brought them into this world, and they are counting on you to show them how to navigate through life. It takes your time, patience and talent to do this. Use your creative nature to work with them and stop scolding them. You are bruising them. Instead, love on them with your time, your hugs and kisses. After you have filled the love tanks of your home, the rest is for your work in the world as an employee, businesswoman, friend and family member. Let go of the junk and let the beauty of my presence in your life serve others.

You, my daughter, are amazing. You have so much to offer. So many are looking to you as a pioneer. As a leader. As a coach. As a friend. As a family member. Get to work.

Selah.

* * *

How does this sit with you? What can you take away that speaks to you and your situation?

_____

_____

_____

_____

_____

_____

_____

_____

_____

How do you recover when you are in the heat of the moment?

_____

_____

_____

_____

_____

_____

_____

_____

Daughter, it's okay to shed tears and feel the emotions you feel. In fact, I want you to speak them out loud to me. Tell me all about your troubles. Know that I will hear your cry and I will hasten unto you.

With love,
Your Heavenly Father

Appendix B: A Word from the Lord

Daughter, daughter, daughter...can't you see this is the attack of the enemy? He wants to make you feel shame. He wants to make you feel incapable when you make a mistake. You are not the only one to make a mistake. I love how you own everything, and you look for opportunities to be and do better. However, I don't like the agony you put yourself through as you face the consequences of your mistakes. It will be well. Remember, as a child of the Most High God, I have the final say.

No matter how it looks to the human eye, no matter what the circumstances are around you, I got you. Throw up your hands and surrender. Trust me and let me fight your battles. The forces are too strong for you to handle in your own strength. Keep talking to me through this. Read your Word as a reminder. Reflect on what you can learn from the situation and use that knowledge moving forward. I am equipping you with tools you will need to do my work. These things you are learning are going to be shared in such a powerful way because you have lived them. I know it doesn't feel good. I know it's hard to not feel shame. I know it's hard not to feel like you are the only one. I know that it's tough, my daughter. But I promise you, I got you.

Do you trust me? Through me, you find strength. Trust me. I will restore the joy of your heart. Selah!

Made in the USA
Middletown, DE
24 September 2020